"*Cognition in Education* is a useful primer for both students and teachers about learning—how it happens and how to improve it. The authors have struck a good balance, with just enough theory to understand and appreciate the practical learning and study strategies and tips described. The chapter on comprehension is particularly helpful and rich with ideas and examples. I especially appreciated the included glossary—all in all, the book is a great resource and an appropriate supplement for many courses."

—**Anita Woolfolk Hoy**, *Professor Emerita,*
The Ohio State University

Cognition

in Education

There is a commonly held belief that some people learn better than others because they are born with stronger abilities. However, research indicates that many high-achieving learners use effective strategies and techniques to improve their learning. These strategies and techniques can be taught to students and inform how we can promote learning. Written by leading experts on learning, this book situates this topic within the broader context of educational psychology research and brings it to a wider audience. With chapters on how the mind works, evidence-based recommendations about how to enhance learning from both student and teacher perspectives, and clear explanations of key learning concepts and ideas, this concise volume is designed for any education course that includes learning in the curriculum. It is indispensable for pre- and in-service teachers and student researchers alike.

Matthew T. McCrudden is Associate Professor in the School of Education at Victoria University of Wellington, New Zealand.

Danielle S. McNamara is Professor in the Department of Psychology at Arizona State University, USA.

Ed Psych Insights

Series Editor: Patricia A. Alexander

Assessment of Student Achievement
Gavin T. L. Brown

Self-Efficacy and Future Goals in Education
Barbara A. Greene

Self-Regulation in Education
Jeffrey A. Greene

Strategic Processing in Education
Daniel L. Dinsmore

Cognition in Education
Matthew T. McCrudden and Danielle S. McNamara

Emotions at School
Reinhard Pekrun, Krista R. Muis, Anne C. Frenzel, and Thomas Goetz

Teacher Expectations in Education
Christine Rubie-Davies

MATTHEW T. McCRUDDEN
AND DANIELLE S. McNAMARA

Cognition
in Education

NEW YORK AND LONDON

First published 2018
by Routledge
711 Third Avenue, New York, NY 10017

and by Routledge
2 Park Square, Milton Park, Abingdon, Oxon, OX14 4RN

Routledge is an imprint of the Taylor & Francis Group, an informa business

Library of Congress Cataloging-in-Publication Data
A catalog record for this book has been requested

ISBN: 978-1-138-22954-9 (hbk)
ISBN: 978-1-138-22953-2 (pbk)
ISBN: 978-1-315-38908-0 (ebk)

Typeset in Joanna MT
by Apex CoVantage, LLC

Contents

Introduction to Human Cognition

One

INTRODUCTION AND OVERVIEW

Along with death and taxes, **learning** is ubiquitous. While we cannot escape death, and try to devote as little time as possible to taxes, understanding how we learn can enrich our lives and the lives of others. This is relevant for students of all ages.

Consider this: Has anyone ever taught you how to learn? It is commonly assumed that some people learn better than others because they are born that way. But cognitive scientists have found that many people who learn better are simply more strategic: they use effective strategies that improve memory and learning. Understanding how the mind works and using that knowledge to regulate our thinking (**metacognition**), enables us to focus our energy on strategies and techniques that can enhance our own learning and enable us to facilitate learning in others.

We believe that both students and teachers benefit enormously from understanding how the mind works, and in turn the various ways to enhance learning. Hence, our overarching goal in *Cognition in Education* is to provide a basic overview of **cognition** (i.e., cognitive processes or mental actions that affect how our minds function) along with usable strategies and evidence-based recommendations for enhancing learning. We adopted three main goals in writing this book: (1) to help our readers understand the science of cognitive psychology and its relevance to education, (2) to describe what is known about the role that cognitive processes play in learning, and (3) to help our readers understand how to apply this knowledge from the perspective of a student and from the perspective of a teacher. Each chapter includes concrete examples, clear definitions of key concepts, and ideas about how to apply these concepts from the perspective of a learner and from the perspective of a teacher or instructor.

A major theme of this book is the beneficial effects of evidence-based, yet inexpensive strategies for learning. We describe a non-exhaustive list of strategies that can greatly improve learning and memory that can be woven into a student's approach to learning and a teacher's approach to instruction. We structured the information on each strategy in the following way: introduce and define the strategy, indicate how the strategy is beneficial to learning, provide evidence to demonstrate the strategy's effectiveness, and describe how knowledge of the strategy can be applied both from a student's perspective and from a teacher's perspective.

Readers will notice that we describe the research studies that provide evidence for the effectiveness of each strategy or technique. We did this because we wanted readers to see some of the evidence behind the presumably beneficial effect of the strategy. It is important for students and teachers to be aware of and seek evidence that is used to support the recommendation for the use of learning strategies. We have selected what we consider to be comprehensible examples of research studies; however, we should note that the strategy recommendations are not based solely on these specific studies. Rather, these recommendations are based on decades of research. In deciding which research studies to present, we sought to identify studies that had clear and strong research designs. This was important because we wanted readers who do not have extensive knowledge of research design to be able to understand what happened in the study, to be able to interpret the findings of the study, and to have confidence that the findings are credible.

Keep in mind that when researchers design a study, they sometimes create situations that differ from how you typically study. For example, let's consider research that we discuss in Chapter 3 that demonstrates the benefits of retrieval practice: *recalling information from memory is more effective than re-reading information*. However, when you prepare for an important test, it is unlikely that you would read a chapter from your assigned text and then attempt to recall the information a week before taking the test, but not look at the information again. You are likely to study the information in some way in the days leading up to the test. Nonetheless, researchers have to design these types of studies to investigate how certain cognitive processes operate and to rule out other factors that may affect learning. As a student, you are more likely to use a combination of strategies.

We describe several strategies in this book. Our list of strategies is not meant to be exhaustive; rather, we aimed to discuss strategies that have consistently been shown to improve learning and memory across a range of research studies, over several decades, and across different age groups, settings, and content. Further, we sought to identify strategies that are inexpensive to use, with respect to time and financial investment. We selected these strategies and techniques because they are strongly supported by evidence and they can be used by most students and teachers.

One important consideration that we do not discuss in this book is the use of technologies in the classroom. We do not do so because we limited this book to techniques that can be implemented inexpensively and with relative ease in the classroom, independently of contemporary technologies. However, the use of technology to provide instruction is increasing across the globe. Many or most educational technologies focus on providing content instruction—they provide means for learning mathematics, science, history, and so on. Nonetheless, such technologies can facilitate the use of strategies that we describe in this book, such as retrieval practice, because among other facilities, they provide platforms for administering quizzes and questions. They can also motivate students, particularly if they are interactive and adaptive (i.e., intelligent) or couched within games. There are, however, fewer technologies that provide adaptive instruction in the realms of reading and writing, and even fewer technologies that focus on teaching strategies, but there are some exceptions.[1,2]

The focus of our book is on how strategies related to *individual* cognition can benefit learning and memory. In particular, we focus in-depth on memory, attention, encoding retrieval, and comprehension. Clearly, cognition in education encompasses a wide range of topics that include reasoning, metacognition, self-regulated learning, problem-solving, peer instruction, collaborative learning, reading, and writing. A separate book could be written about each of these topics. In some cases, these topics are included in other books in this series and we encourage readers to consider those resources, as well as a multitude of other available resources.

We begin this book by providing an overview of cognition, with a particular focus on human memory. In Chapter 1, we use a general information processing model of human cognition to provide an organizing framework for the memory systems that comprise cognition and how various cognitive processes connect the memory systems. Although there are different information processing models in the literature, they share some common features. We focus on these common features, rather than one particular model, because they provide a useable representation of human memory that we believe is understandable and consistent with theory and evidence about learning. Further, the organizing framework we present in this book is compatible with other models of cognition that students may encounter in their courses. In the remaining sections of this chapter, we provide general overviews of the information processing model, working memory, and long-term memory. We believe that knowledge of different types of memory systems and how they are connected can enable students and teachers to develop a better understanding of how different strategies and techniques can be beneficial for learning. Further, an understanding of how memory works prepares the reader for the information that is covered in the following chapters.

In Chapter 2, we discuss attention and preparing to learn. Attention is a crucial cognitive process that 'ignites' learning. To think about something, we have to pay attention to it, and whatever we pay attention to dominates our thoughts. However, our attention is limited. Thus, in Chapter 2 we discuss ways to ensure that we attend to information that helps us learn—and to avoid attending to information that distracts us from learning.

In Chapter 3, we discuss ways to improve memory and focus on two key strategies: distributed practice (i.e., spreading out study activities over time) and retrieval practice (attempting to retrieve previously learned information from memory). We discuss how encoding via distributed practice can be used to create and update long-term memory and how retrieval practice can be used to strengthen the accessibility of long-term memory. We focused on distributed practice and retrieval practice in particular because they are inexpensive and can be widely applied. Further, there is strong evidence that they are effective: (1) they benefit students of different ages and abilities, (2) they have been shown to be beneficial to students learning on a variety of outcome measures, and (3) they have been shown to be beneficial in a variety of educational contexts.

In Chapters 2 and 3, we discuss several techniques for improving attention and memory. But, what if you don't understand the content? In Chapter 4, we discuss ways to improve comprehension and focus on three key strategies: generating questions, elaborating and explaining information, and completing **graphic organizers**. What these three strategies have in common is that they all involve the learner actively generating information in the attempt to create meaning. We discuss these strategies in particular because there is substantial evidence that these strategies are beneficial to comprehension across a range of tasks, learning outcomes, and age groups.

Information Processing Model of Human Cognition

In the remainder of this chapter, we discuss memory and cognition and how they can affect learning.

First, we discuss the information processing model of human cognition. Then we briefly describe working memory and long-term memory, including the distinction between **declarative memory** and **procedural memory**.

The first stage of information processing requires sensation. **Sensory memory** is the memory system that passively detects environmental stimuli that impact our senses. It is a brief record (i.e., two seconds or less) that allows us to subsequently transform our sensory experiences into meaningful forms. For example, our ears detect vibrations and the brain transforms them into sounds that we can comprehend. Our eyes detect light, which the brain can transform into images that we interpret.

While sensory memory is involved in the brief retention of *sensory experience*, **working memory** is the memory system that we use to consciously hold and process *information* for short periods of time (i.e., about 20 seconds). **Long-term memory** is the memory system that enables us to retain *information* for long periods of time, such as days, weeks, and even years.

Attention is our ability to focus on specific stimuli, ideas, or events for further processing in working memory, and we can control where we direct our focus of attention. For simplicity's sake, let's say that information can be held at three basic levels of *activation* (see Figure 1.1).

One, information is activated, which means it reaches the level of conscious awareness. It has a high 'electrical charge' and is in our focus of attention (represented in Figure 1.1 by the circle in the middle labelled "Activated"). Information in the focus of attention can come from the environment via sensory memory, from long-term memory via reactivation, or both. When we hold and process information in our focus of attention, we are using working memory.

Two, information is in a heightened state of activation, but is below the level of conscious awareness, which means it has the potential to be available with additional electrical charge. That is, is has a moderate electrical charge and is currently outside our focus of attention (represented in Figure 1.1 by the light grey box labelled "Moderately Activated").

Three, information is available in long-term memory, but it has limited or no electrical charge so it is not currently accessible and it outside our focus of attention (represented in Figure 1.1 by the dark grey box labelled "Not Activated").

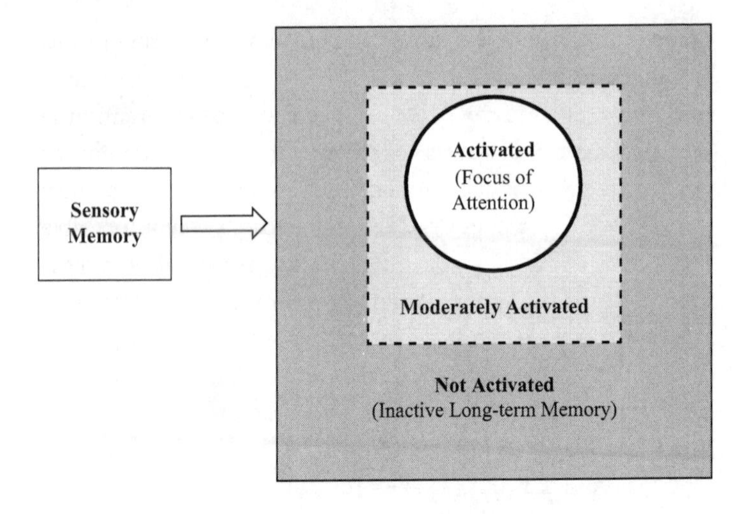

Figure 1.1 Three basic levels of information activation in human cognition

We can focus our attention on stimuli from our surrounding environment, our internal thoughts and ideas, or both. When we focus our attention on stimuli from our surrounding environment, the stimuli are initially captured by sensory memory. Alternatively, when we focus our attention on ideas already known, the information is activated or retrieved from long-term memory. This allows us to reflect upon, update, or use what we already know. When we focus on both sensory experience that is comprehensible and ideas that have been activated from long-term memory, we are able to use what we know to make sense of our experiences.

When we study, one of our primary goals is to use the information we are learning for some purpose in the future. To do this, we need to be able to retain the information in long-term memory. The good news is that long-term memory has a large, if not limitless, capacity. The cliffhanger, however, is that not all of the information that is in long-term memory is easily ***accessible***. Have you ever had the feeling that you know something, but you just could not remember it? This is because information may be ***available*** in long-term memory, but it may not be immediately or easily accessible. By analogy, a book may be available in your university library, but you may not be able to access it without knowing the reference code or the physical layout of the library. Thus, information may be available in memory, although it may be difficult to access or retrieve.

> ***Availability*** *refers to whether information is present in memory.*
> ***Accessibility*** *refers to the extent to which information is retrievable.*

Obviously, this is problematic if and when you need to use the information. The extent to which information is available and accessible depends on both how it was *encoded* and how it is being *retrieved*. Importantly, the presence of retrieval cues plays a crucial role in our ability to activate information in memory. **Encoding** refers to the processes we use to transform information into a memory representation, which can then be retained in long-term memory over time. Encoding involves using our current experiences to create new memories. **Retrieval** refers to the activation of information that is already retained in long-term memory.

We can encode information in many different ways, but some ways are more effective than others in creating long-term memories. For example, we can attempt to learn information by repeating it over and over, relying very little on **prior knowledge**, a process known as rote or maintenance rehearsal. This approach can work in some cases, but it is relatively ineffective. It involves passive rehearsal of information. Alternatively, we can attempt to explain or discuss the new information, integrating the new information with what we already know, which involves a process known as elaborative rehearsal. For example, if you were told that penguins carry their eggs on the top of their feet, you might use your prior knowledge that penguins live in an icy habitat and that it is important to keep eggs warm. You might then reason that carrying the eggs on top of their feet would help to keep the eggs off the ice and keep them warm. Actively using prior knowledge from long-term memory to process and understand new information helps to *connect* new information to ideas already known. Hence, you would be much more likely to remember this new information if you explained it to yourself or to someone else than if you simply repeated it over and over. Generating explanations creates connections. And, making connections between what you already know what you are learning is perhaps the most important factor that influences the success of encoding, and in turn, enhances learning and memory. In sum, there are different ways of encoding information and not all forms of encoding are equally effective in creating long-term memories. We elaborate on how students can create those connections in more detail in Chapters 3 and 4.

Importantly, the act of retrieving information from memory actually strengthens memory. For instance, if you study something one day and then attempt to retrieve the information the next day, you can strengthen your memory for that information just by practicing retrieval of that information. As we mentioned earlier, we elaborate on this topic in more detail in Chapter 3. Simply put, retrieving information from memory improves your ability to retrieve it again in the future. Thus, retrieval plays a crucial role in learning. In sum:

Connecting new information to prior knowledge enhances encoding.
Repeated retrieval reinforces access to information in long-term memory.

CONSCIOUSNESS OR WORKING MEMORY

Whatever you are currently thinking about, your conscious awareness, is referred to as working memory. But there is more to working memory than just conscious awareness. **Working memory** is the memory system that enables us to actively *hold* and *process* information over a short time frame (10–20 seconds). For example, when you mentally multiply 14 × 4, you have to mentally hold various numbers and process computations of those numbers. As you can see, working memory plays a crucial role in learning.

A defining feature of working memory is that there is a time limit for how long we can maintain and process information in conscious awareness without continually rehearsing the information (**limited duration assumption**). As time passes, some of the information incrementally loses activation in the absence of rehearsal until it disappears from conscious awareness altogether. Further, new or additional information may be competing for 'space' in working memory. Given the limited amount of time that information can remain active in working memory and the limited amount of information that can be in our focus of attention (**limited capacity assumption**), it is crucial that we have the ability to retain information for longer periods of time in long-term memory. Later in this book, we will discuss ways to maximize long-term learning given these limitations on our working memory resources. But next, we describe long-term memory in greater detail.

LONG-TERM MEMORY

A fundamental goal of education is to provide instruction that helps students not just attend to information, but also to remember and use it for long periods of time.

> *Long-term memory is the memory system that retains information for long periods of time.*

Long-term memory contrasts with working memory, which is relatively fleeting. We often attend to things that are not remembered for more than a few seconds or minutes. But, merely attending to information in working memory does little good in the long run. Thus, the ultimate goal is to retain information in long-term memory for longer periods. That's learning.

Long-term memory has a seemingly *limitless capacity*. That is, it does not appear as though there is a maximum amount of information that can be retained in long-term memory. So, the problem is not how much information can be retained, but how to improve retention and retrieval. Various ways to enhance retention and retrieval from long-term memory are discussed later in the book.

In this section, we discuss two types of long-term memory: declarative memory and procedural memory.

> **Declarative memory** is our ability to state and use facts and concepts.
>
> **Procedural memory** is our ability to perform actions or skills that we learn when we acquire procedures.

These two types of memory are related to how we learn information and skills, and how we retain them.

Declarative Memory

Who won the 100-meter dash in the 2016 Olympics? The straightforward answer to this question is Usain Bolt, from Jamaica. Did you happen to watch the race and recall seeing it? Suppose you watched it and that you recall who you were with, where you were, the time of day, and your reaction to the finish. Your ability to recall the winner of the race and your ability to recall seeing the race are both instances of declarative memory. **Declarative memory** is our ability to state and use facts and concepts.

In general, there are two types of declarative memory. The first is **semantic memory**. This is general knowledge of the world. In our example, recalling the winner of the race would be an instance of semantic memory. However, semantic memory is more sophisticated than a collection of facts. It represents your conceptual knowledge and general understanding of the world. It includes your knowledge of words, various objects and features of the environment, your perceptions of the world around you, and ideas that you acquire and refine over the course of your lifetime. For example, knowing that the word "water" refers to a liquid is part of semantic memory. Similarly, knowing that water is satisfying when you are thirsty, is used to make tea, is slippery when it is frozen, can burn when it's boiled, and is salty when in the ocean all constitute semantic memory. Thus, semantic memory encompasses much of what we know and enables us to interact with the world.

The second type of declarative memory is **episodic memory**. This is memory for personal experiences or events. In our example, recalling who you were with, where you were, or your emotional reaction to the event is considered episodic memory. A defining feature of episodic memory is that consists of personally experienced events. Each event includes you (the self). You are the actor, recipient, or observer of some action and your perspective plays a key role in what you remember about an event. Further, it may include your emotional or physiological reaction to an event.

In our initial example about the 100-meter dash, you can see that the experience of watching the race contributed to both semantic and episodic memory. Similarly, perhaps you know that water is slippery when frozen because you once fell on an icy sidewalk outside your house as a child, or when you tried to ice skate for the first time at a nearby hockey rink or the neighborhood pond. Memory that originates from the joint contribution of semantic and episodic memory is known as **autobiographical memory**.

For the purposes of this book, we highlight the distinction between semantic and episodic memory because students' existing memories play a crucial role in current and future learning. David Ausubel, an influential and respected scholar in educational psychology, once claimed, "If I had to reduce all of educational psychology to just one principle, it would say this: 'The most important single factor influencing learning is what the learner already knows.'" Students are largely asked to learn semantic knowledge for the purpose of developing semantic memory. However, given the influence of previous knowledge on current learning, it is important to build links not only to students' prior *semantic* memory, but also to their prior *episodic* memory. Students bring their experiences to the learning context and we should capitalize on what they already know both in and out of formal educational settings to support learning.

How might we do this? One possibility is to use real-world examples to help students connect semantic knowledge to their personal experiences in episodic memory. For instance, to help students understand the limitations of working memory, you could ask them if they have ever been introduced to a group of 8–9 people at a party and found it difficult to remember the names of the people in the group? This real-world example can help students connect semantic knowledge about the limitations of working memory (i.e., we can only hold a limited amount of information at any given time) to their personal experiences in episodic memory (i.e., memory for an experience at a party in which it was difficult to remember peoples' names).

However, the real-world examples you introduce in class may not pertain to all students if they have not had these experiences. What happens if students do not have episodic memory to be linked to semantic memory? Create it! Give students the opportunity to personally experience events that help them learn semantic knowledge. For instance, suppose elementary students are learning about gravity in a physical science course and the spinal cord in a life science class. Their teacher could ask them to record their height every morning and every evening for a week then bring the measurements to class. The students could create graphs or tables to depict the data, and the teacher could have students identify trends in the data. In general, the students should note that they are slightly taller in the morning than in the evening. This experience could be used to link episodic memory ("I am taller in the morning") to semantic knowledge in their physical science class (i.e., gravity is an invisible force that acts on us) or in their life science class (i.e., what is the structure and function of vertebral discs in the spinal column?). When students personally experience an event, the experience can be used to support semantic memory about course content.

The content that students are generally asked to learn is semantic in nature. However, leveraging students' existing knowledge, including both semantic and episodic memory in long-term memory, can help them develop greater mastery of semantic knowledge.

Procedural Memory

How do you tie your shoes, ride a bike, or swim in a pool? The ability to do these tasks involves the use of **procedural memory**—our ability to perform actions or skills. For example, when learning to ride a bike, we learn procedures that enable us to cycle down a road, through a forest, or over a mountain. Once we learn the procedures (e.g., balancing, pedaling, turning, shifting gears, braking), we can bike automatically, investing little or no conscious thought to the execution of these procedures, even though we may consciously decide to do them. A primary way to measure or assess procedural memory is to observe a person perform a skill, or to perform a skill yourself.

In some instances, it is possible to verbally explain elements of procedural memory. For instance, when solving a math problem a person can explain the steps involved in computing a solution. Similarly, while reading a text passage, a person can consciously ask questions about the text while reading, such as the meaning of each word, the parts of speech that compose the sentences (e.g., nouns, verbs, determiners), the structure of the sentences (e.g., noun phrases, verb phrases), and the meaning of the sentences. In both of these examples, the person is verbally explaining procedural memory while performing a cognitive action. This can also occur when a person is performing a physical action, such as writing the letter "A" or driving a car. Whether the action is cognitive, physical, or both, a person utilizes procedural memory to perform the skill, while at the same time using declarative memory to verbally explain elements of the procedure.

However, in many cases it is difficult to verbally explain how to perform a skill. For instance, it is difficult to explain how you balance on a bike or float while swimming across a pool. This requires the coordination and automation of numerous skills. For this reason, procedural memory is often considered to have explicit and implicit characteristics. **Explicit procedural memory** consists of actions you can describe. In the examples above about solving a math problem or writing the letter "A", this can involve both cognitive and physical actions. **Implicit procedural memory** consists of actions you can perform, such as balancing on a bike or floating while swimming.

We highlight this distinction between explicit and implicit procedural memory because procedural memory may begin as explicit memory when a person is learning to do an action. It is believed that procedural memory for an action develops in three main stages. In the first stage, the declarative stage, a person develops an explicit understanding of the task, including different components of the skill and the basic procedures a person needs to follow. In the second stage, the associative stage, a person repeatedly practices the skill. Patterns that lead to more successful outcomes are repeated and become strengthened with repeated practice. The third and final stage is automaticity. Automaticity involves performing an action with little or no conscious thought. For example, if you are a licensed driver, you likely do not have to think consciously about pressing the clutch or the accelerator. Likewise, you are probably an expert reader, who has practiced reading for more than 10 years. If so, you can read these words and sentences without having to look up each word in a dictionary, and without thought to the structure of the sentences. The amount of practice necessary to automate procedures depends on the complexity of the skill as well as the level of performance that you are seeking—more complex skills such as reading and writing take years of practice, compared to riding a bike or driving a car. But driving in a Formula One race or riding in the Tour de France require years of practice.

Procedural memory is particularly relevant to the strategies that we discuss throughout this book. In this book, we describe strategies and techniques that can help students remember information and comprehend challenging content. Providing students with this information about these strategies may be the first step, but that is not enough! Student must have practice using the strategies until strategy use becomes automatic. Practice in using strategies is key to becoming an effective learner.

In Chapters 3 and 4, we further discuss memory and techniques to improve learning. But before we do this, let's look at attention in more detail in Chapter 2.

HUMAN COGNITION: SUMMARY OF KEY IDEAS

1. Sensory memory is the memory system that passively detects environmental stimuli that impact our senses.
2. Working memory is a limited capacity system that enables us to actively hold and process information over brief time frames.
3. Long-term memory is a limitless capacity system that enables us to retain information for long periods of time, such as days, weeks, and even years.
4. Attention is our ability to focus on specific stimuli, ideas, or events for further processing in working memory.
5. Information can be held at three basic levels of activation: activated (attention and working memory), moderately activated, and relatively inactive (inactive portion of long-term memory).
6. Information can be available in long-term memory, but it may or may not be accessible (i.e., retrievable).
7. Encoding is the creation of new memories, and retrieval is the activation of information that is already retained in long-term memory.
8. Retrieval is important because connecting new information to prior knowledge enhances encoding, and repeated retrieval reinforces access to information in long-term memory.

9. There are two types of long-term memory: declarative memory and procedural memory.
10. There are two types of declarative memory: semantic memory and episodic memory.
11. The joint contribution of semantic and episodic memory is known as autobiographical memory.
12. Procedural memory can be either explicit or implicit.

Attention and Preparing to Learn

Two

In this chapter, we discuss attention and how it can affect learning. First, we discuss the limitations of attention. Then, we focus on ways to help students pay attention to information that helps them learn and to avoid attending to information that distracts from learning. Students are more likely to attend to stimuli that are:

- novel, emotional, or physically distinct, and
- personally relevant.

There is so much going on all around us! Look around a room and from the corners of your eyes, you might see several people, a room full of furniture, cars, birds, clouds, or planes. We process so much, and yet we remember so little! How can we understand these basic processes of taking in information from the world, attending to information, and then remembering all that we need to remember?

These are questions that cognitive psychologists have been asking for well over a half of a century. Decades of research have been dedicated to understanding how we navigate the world using a multitude of sensations and how we attend to some sensations, but not others.

For example, when you walk across a university campus on your way to class, you encounter many sights and sounds. Imagine posters about upcoming events plastered onto billboards, other students walking to class, cyclists and skateboarders weaving through the traffic, and students playing Frisbee on a greenspace. Your mind is focused, in part, on getting to class, but you also focus on your surroundings. A flyer on a billboard may catch your eye. Bad Religion is coming to town. If you have not heard of them, you may think: "Who are those guys? What kind of name is that for a band?" Or, if you are a fan, you may think, "Greg Graffin is a great lyricist. When is the show and how much are tickets? I hope I can go." Out of the corner of your eye, you spot a cyclist who passes you. "She's going pretty fast. She's asking for trouble without a helmet." As you walk past the greenspace, you may think, "I could never throw a Frisbee that well. They make it look so easy!" In each of these examples, stimuli from the environment influenced your immediate thoughts. However, suppose you have a test that day in your class. Your thoughts may be preoccupied with the test and you may take little notice of billboards, cyclists/skateboarders, or Frisbees. In this situation, your goals, present activities, and prior knowledge predominantly occupy your immediate thoughts. Importantly, whatever the case, only a subset of information from these sources enters into conscious awareness at any given time. That is, we focus our attention on some stimuli to the exclusion of others.

ATTENTION

Attention refers to our ability to focus on specific stimuli or events for further processing. The defining feature of attention is that it has a limited capacity (**limited capacity assumption**); only a limited amount of information can be in our focus of attention at any given time.

Our Attention Is Limited!

That is, we can only focus on a limited amount of stimuli, ideas, or events at any given time. For instance, you cannot successfully drive a car and read a text simultaneously; rather, you can only successfully attend to one or the other. Similarly, you cannot successfully comprehend two spoken messages that occur at the same time.

Consider again Figure 1.1 in Chapter 1 (shown again in this chapter). Attention is represented as the circle in the middle. It is helpful to think of attention as a *spotlight* that is directed towards a stage during a performance, such as a play. The stage is wide and has different performers and props on it. However, the spotlight is directed towards some of the performers and props, whereas the others are outside of the spotlight. That is, only a portion of the stage is inside the focus of attention, your thoughts are directed towards what the actors are saying or doing and your interpretations of these actions.

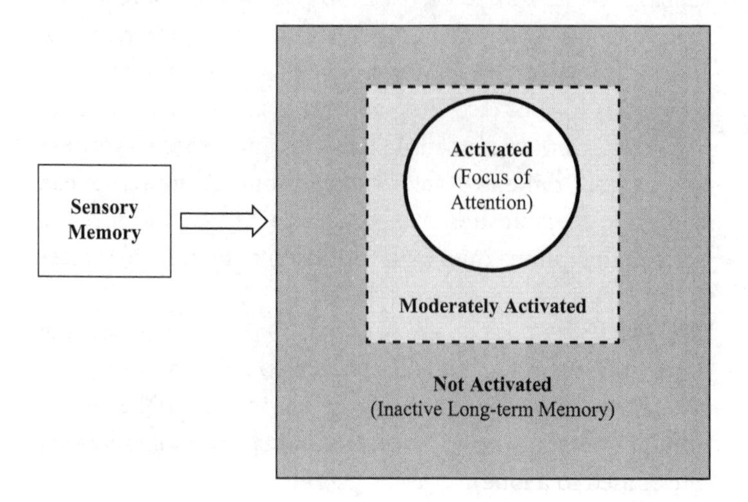

Figure 1.1 Three basic levels of information activation in human cognition

There are three basic levels of information activation in human cognition illustrated in Figure 1.1. In this chapter, we focus on attention, which can be thought of as the *activated* portion of long-term memory, or the *spotlight/focus* of attention.

A research study by E. Colin Cherry[3] published in 1953 illustrates the limited capacity of attention. In this study, participants listened via headphones to spoken messages. But there was a twist; both messages were about different topics and were played at the same time. One message was played into the headphone on one ear, and a different message was played into the headphone on the participant's other ear. The participants' task was to repeat aloud or "shadow," as they listened to it, the message in one ear without making any errors and to ignore the message that was played into the other ear. Cherry reasoned that if attention has a limited capacity, then attending to one message would prevent people from attending to the other message. What did he find? First, all participants successfully "shadowed" the message in the specified ear. Thus, he had evidence that participants had successfully attended to that message.

But that was only part of the picture. The crucial question was whether attending to the message in the specified ear came at the expense of the message in the other ear. To answer this question, participants were asked to provide information about the message from the *unattended* ear after the listening task.

What were the participants able to report from the unattended ear? They were able to report:

- If a voice was present (i.e., a person was speaking as opposed to a tone).
- If the voice changed to a higher pitch.
- If the voice was replaced by a tone.

These are all **physical properties** of the message. What were the participants NOT able to report from the unattended ear? They were *not* able to report:

- The content of message (e.g., the topic).
- The language of message (e.g., English vs. French).
- A change in the language of message.
- Whether the message was speech vs. nonsense backward speech.

In sum, the results showed that participants had no memory for the meaning of the message that was played in the unattended ear or for any words from that message. Further, they did not notice whether the unattended message was in a different language. They were only able to report on non-semantic characteristics of the message.

This study led to two main conclusions. The first conclusion was that attention has a limited capacity. When given two separate messages, people only have enough capacity available to attend to one of the messages in a meaningful way. The second conclusion was that we have some control over our attention. When people are asked to attend to only one of the messages, they are able to do so.

The fact that attention has limited capacity has implications for our ability to successfully do tasks in the real world. Imagine having a conversation on your cell phone while you are driving. Does talking on a cell phone while driving affect driving performance? A research study conducted by David Strayer, Frank Drews, and William Johnston[4] addressed this question. Participants did a computerized simulated driving task (which of course is safer and more ethical) that included a series of events, such as responding to a braking vehicle. The researchers measured how long it took participants to react to these events. To test whether talking on a cell phone affected participants' driving performance, the participants did the driving task either with or without having hands-free phone conversation about an interesting topic. If talking on a cell phone interferes with driving performance, then drivers should perform worse when driving and talking than when just driving. What did the evidence show? People made more errors (e.g., rear-ended braking vehicles, failed to see signs) and took longer to carry out tasks when having a phone conversation while driving compared to driving without talking on the phone, particularly in high density traffic. The finding that performance differed with and without talking on the phone further highlights the limited capacity of attention, and confirms that we should not use our cell phones while driving.

Moreover, did you know that people who drive and talk on their cell phones *are four times* more likely to have an accident than people who are not using their cell phones while driving? Interestingly, people who drive intoxicated are *four times* more likely to have an accident than people who have not consumed alcohol. Therefore, talking on a cell phone while driving can be just as dangerous as drinking and driving!

ATTENTION AND LEARNING

Attention plays a key role in learning; it allows us to focus our thoughts on particular ideas. We cannot think about something unless we pay attention to it, and whatever we pay attention to will dominate our thinking. However, attention has a limited capacity, and information that detracts from learning can compete with information that facilitates learning for these limited attentional resources. Therefore, to promote learning, students must:

1. pay attention to information that helps them learn, and
2. avoid attending to information that distracts them from learning.

Doing this helps students focus their limited attentional resources effectively. In the next sections, we'll discuss stimuli that gain attention, provide examples of how the knowledge can be applied, and provide research-based evidence to support these ideas.

People Focus Their Attention on Things That Are Novel, Emotional, or Physically Distinct

Cognitive psychologists have found that we focus our attention on stimuli that are **novel** or stand out in some way. For instance, how difficult is it to ignore someone's accent? When you and your friends are from a similar geographical location, you typically have the same accent. However, suppose you meet someone whose accent is clearly distinct from your accent. You notice this almost immediately. As the person speaks, you may find yourself asking, "It doesn't sound like she's from here. I wonder where she grew up?" The point is, people focus their attention on stimuli that are novel to a greater extent than stimuli that are less distinct.

Emotional content also gains attention. For example, at the cinema, previews for coming attractions contain many of the best parts of a movie. Why? The studio believes that filling the preview with the funniest, scariest, and most exciting parts of a movie, will gain your attention, and hope that you will go see the movie. Emotional content is a natural attention-getter.

The physical properties of a stimulus can also capture our attention. Why do some "roadwork ahead" signs or railroad crossing signs have blinking lights? Blinking lights are designed to alert drivers to upcoming hazards. They are impossible to ignore and are meant to prompt drivers to think, "What's going on up ahead?" and to proceed with caution. Physical properties such as contrast, color, and movement capture attention.

The physical properties of our speech can also capture attention. When people have conversations or any form of spontaneous speech, they use pauses or hesitations such as 'uh' and 'uhm' between some of their words. Interestingly, listeners are sensitive to these pauses and use them to comprehend speech. Listeners raise their attention to speech that follows pauses and this can actually be beneficial for their memory.

A study by Hans Bosker and several colleagues[5] shows how voice contrast can gain attention. Participants listened to short passages that sometimes contained a filled pause (e.g., ". . . that the patient with the *uh* wound was . . ."). After listening to each passage, they gave the participants a transcript of the passage. The transcript was either exactly the same as the speech, or it had one word in the transcript that had been substituted. For instance, in the phrase ". . . that the patient with the uh wound was . . .," the word *wound* was replaced by the word *injury*. Then, the participants were asked to indicate whether the transcript corresponded with the speech. Participants more accurately recalled words from the previously heard speech when the word was preceded by a pause or hesitation. Thus, changes in speech can gain students' attention.

People Focus Their Attention on Relevant Stimuli

Do you pay close attention to "for sale" signs in the front of houses? Do you look intently at houses, focusing your thoughts on the location, number of rooms, and size of the yard? If you aren't looking to buy a house, your answer is probably "no." You might not even notice "for sale" signs because houses are not personally relevant to you.

Relevance is the extent to which information is useful to a person's goals. Relevance can focus attention. Before you have kids, you may have no idea how many houses are for sale. Things may change with the impending arrival of a child. Suddenly, houses become relevant to your life because you need more space. Consequently, you focus on houses whenever you pass one on the street. The point is, when something is relevant to us, it more easily gains our attention. And, once we attend to something, it can prompt certain kinds of thoughts. For example, a "for sale" sign might prompt you to think, "I wonder if that house has a backyard," or "How long will it take to get to work from there?" Having those kinds of thoughts begins the process of connecting new information to what you already know, and making connections in memory.

Hence, relevance is particularly important to learning. When a lesson is relevant to students, they are more likely to pay attention, and in turn, learn the material. One technique to increase relevance for a student is by giving students **task-orienting instructions**.

Let's look at a research study that demonstrated the effects of pre-reading instructions on attention and memory. One such study was conducted by Matt. McCrudden, Joe Magliano, and Gregg Schraw[6] who asked undergraduate students to read a text passage about four remote countries, including Pitcairn and Honduras. The passage described various features of all of the countries including geography, climate, government, economy, transportation, and language. There were three groups and they were given different instructions before they read. Students in the *Pitcairn* group were asked to imagine they would be living in Pitcairn for several years and to focus on information about Pitcairn. Students in the *Honduras* group were asked to imagine they would be living in Honduras for several years and to focus on information about Honduras. Students in the *control* group were asked to read for understanding. Thus, the researchers investigated whether pre-reading instructions would affect attention during reading. To measure attention, they measured how much time students spent reading information that was and was not relevant to their pre-reading instructions. Further, students took a memory test after they read the passage.

The results showed that participants spent more time reading information that was relevant to their pre-reading instructions (see Figure 2.1). For instance, when students were asked to

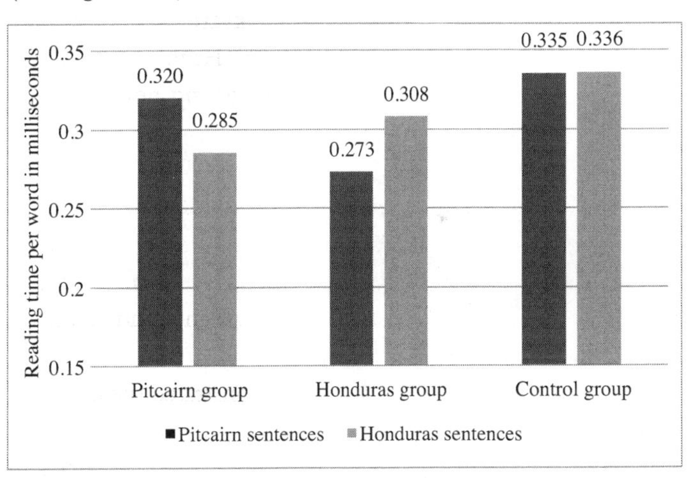

Figure 2.1 The results from McCrudden, Magliano, and Schraw[6] show that students spend more time reading information that is relevant to their task instructions whereas students without specific task instructions (i.e., the control group) do not. (*Reading time is reported in milliseconds per word for the most relevant sentences in the text. Higher scores are indicative of longer, slower reading times*)

focus on information about Pitcairn, they spent more time reading information about Pitcairn than information about Honduras. The same pattern was true for the participants who were asked to focus on Honduras, except they spent more time on information about Honduras. Students in the control group spent the same amount of time reading both types of information. These findings showed that the pre-reading instructions affected students' attention, such that they focused on information that was signaled by the pre-reading instructions.

Further, on the memory test, students remembered more of the information that was signaled by the pre-reading instructions (see Figure 2.2). For instance, when students were asked to focus on information about Pitcairn, they remembered more

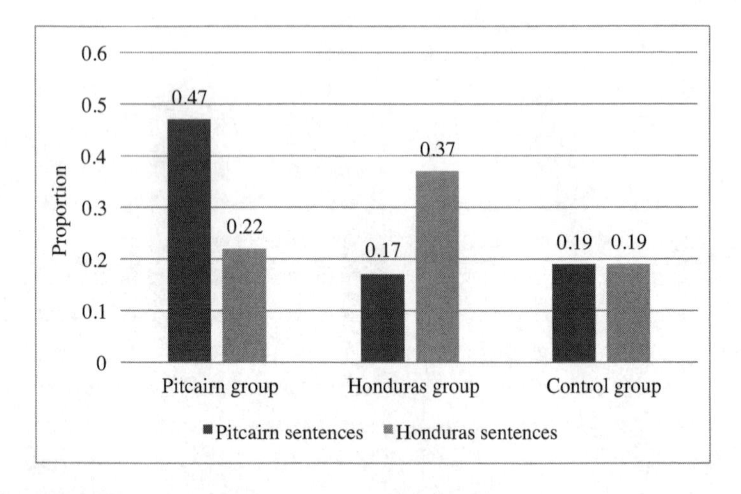

Figure 2.2 The results from McCrudden, Magliano, and Schraw[6] show that students recall more information that is relevant to their task instructions, and remember as much information as the students in control group for information that is not relevant. (*The results are presented in terms of the proportion of recall of the most relevant ideas in the text passage. There were 22 highly relevant ideas for the Pitcairn and 26 for Honduras*)

information about Pitcairn than about Honduras. Interestingly, students in the experimental groups recalled information that was *not* relevant to their pre-reading instructions to the same extent as students in the control group. For instance, the Pitcairn group recalled as much information about Honduras as the control group. Overall, this study showed that students directed more attention to relevant information, remembered more of this information, but this did not impede their recall of information that was not targeted by their pre-reading instructions. Thus, task focusing instructions can help students direct their attention to relevant information and it can help them remember this information better.

Providing *prequestions* is another technique that can influence the relevance of information and help to focus students' attention. Do your textbooks have questions at the start of each chapter? Does your instructor provide questions at the start of class? Evidence indicates that it is a good idea to try to answer these questions. You may be wondering, 'How can I answer these questions before I've encountered the information needed to answer them?' Aren't I reading or attending class to learn something new?' It turns out that attempting to answer questions before you read or at the start of class is beneficial for learning. Let's look at two research studies that illustrate the benefits of answering prequestions.

In the first study, Michael Pressley and several colleagues[7] asked students to answer questions that pertained to one of their chapters for class *before* they actually read the chapter. Students were randomly assigned into one of three groups. Two of the groups received 23 prequestions. One of these groups attempted to answer the prequestions, whereas the other group was asked to determine whether the prequestions made sense. This latter group was included to determine whether mere exposure to the prequestions was enough to affect learning.

The third group did not see the prequestions at all before they read the chapter. After reading the entire chapter, all of the students completed a short-answer test that included 46 items (23 of which were identical to the prequestions).

There were two main findings. The first main finding pertained to the two groups that received prequestions. The researchers compared the scores between these groups of students on the posttest items that were identical to the prequestions. The students who answered prequestions before reading did better on these items at posttest than students who determined whether the questions made sense. This indicated that attempting to answer the prequestions, not merely reading them, was more beneficial for learning. Interestingly, even when the students answered prequestions incorrectly before reading, they still answered more of these questions correctly on the posttest than the students who only read the prequestions. Thus, it turns out that independently of whether you can correctly answer prequestions, the act of attempting to answer them is beneficial for learning. Perhaps this happens because answering prequestions helps students select question-relevant information when they read. Second, performance did not differ across three groups on the items that were not prequestions. This indicated that students did not learn information related to the prequestions at the expense of information that was not related to the prequestions. In other words, answering prequestions enhanced learning of information needed to answer the prequestions, but did not interfere with learning of information that was not needed to answer the prequestions.

Next, let's look at a research study in which students attempted to answer prequestions before they viewed a presentation. In a research study by Shana Carpenter and Alexander Toftness[8] students viewed a video presentation. Students were randomly assigned to one of two groups. The *prequestion* group answered six prequestions about the video presentation they were about to view. That is, they answered questions before they watched a video that included answers to those questions. The *no prequestion* group only watched the video; they did not receive the prequestions before they watched the video.

After the video presentation, both groups answered the same 12 questions about the presentation. There were three main findings. Let's first look at overall test performance between the two groups. The prequestion group answered more items correctly (57%) than the no prequestion group (38%). Thus, the prequestion group outperformed the students who did not answer prequestions before the presentations. Next, let's look at performance *within* the prequestion group (see Figure 2.3).

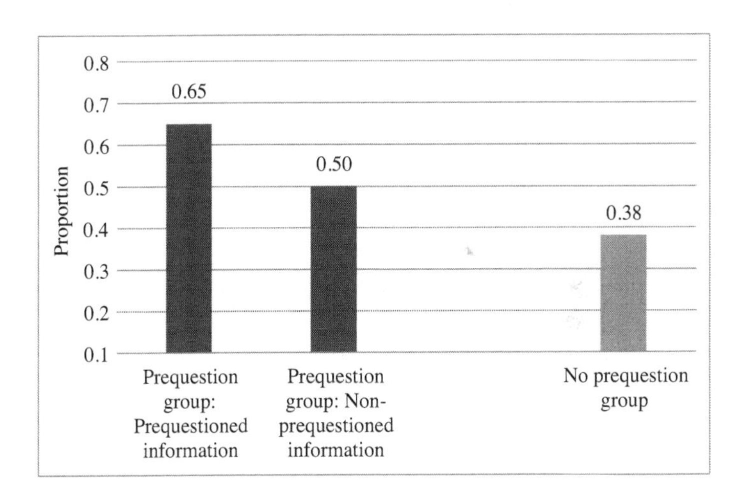

Figure 2.3 The results from Carpenter and Toftness[8] show that students who answer prequestions not only remember more information that is relevant to the prequestions, but also more information that is not relevant to the prequestions compared to students who do not answer prequestions. [*The results are presented in terms of the proportion of correct answers out of 12 [6 items worth 2 points each] for each category of information [i.e., prequestioned and non-prequestioned] for the prequestion group and out of 24 [12 items worth 2 points each] for the non-prequestion group*]

As you would expect, these students had higher scores for the prequestioned items (65%) compared to the non-prequestioned items (50%). Thus, students do better on items that are relevant to prequestions. Lastly, let's look at performance between the two groups on the non-prequestioned items (see Figure 2.3). For the non-prequestion group, all of the items were non-prequestioned. For the prequestion group, half of the items were non-prequestioned. Did answering prequestions also help students learn non-prequestioned information? Final test performance for the non-prequestioned information for the prequestion group (50%) was higher than the non-prequestioned group (38%). Thus, answering prequestions promoted learning of information from the presentation even when that information was not needed to answer the prequestions.

Using Knowledge of Attention: Student Perspective

In this section, we discuss how you can use knowledge of attention as a learner. Several of the examples we use pertain to reading and writing, primarily because these activities are common to many students. However, you may be involved in other activities, and the basic ideas can be transferred to those activities as well.

Reading is an effortful activity and should be done in an environment with minimal distractions. If stimuli from your study environment capture you attention, you will no longer be paying attention to the text information, which can disrupt comprehension and thinking. Thus, it is a good idea to read in a place that has minimal distractions. Trying to read a biology text in your living room while your roommate is watching TV is a less-than-optimal reading environment. There is a stream of sound coming from the TV that may have familiar ideas or voices, commercials may be louder than the show, images on the screen are continually changing, your roommate might ask you questions or may be preparing food or eating. All of these things can capture your attention and direct it away from whatever you are trying to read. One solution is to choose a reading environment that minimizes these types of distractions. Perhaps you could read in a different room or go to a nearby library. Or plan to read when your roommate is gone. Minimizing distractions is crucial to learning!

Another way to help you focus your attention while preparing to learn is to bring all necessary study materials to your study location so that you avoid losing track of your thoughts as you try to search for materials you need to use. If you need to solve math problems, have a calculator and a pencil handy. If you need to write an argument paper, have your outline of the paper and the documents that you will need to communicate your position.

You can make your reading time more productive by noticing the signals writers use to capture your attention. Books often have headings or bold or italicized print to indicate transitions between topics or to signal important ideas, or they may use visual displays to show key ideas. Authors make a special effort to create these signals because they want you to pay attention to them. These are effective ways to gain attention, and textbook editors want to help readers more easily identify important information, so they use these types of devices to help readers.

Going to class is also an important part of being a student. There are ways to make effective use of lecture time. For instance, many first year courses at large universities are taught in large auditoriums with over 300 people in the class. Sitting near the back makes it more difficult to pay attention to the professor. Students in front of you might bring their laptops to class to shop online or to access social media. This can be distracting, particularly if there are moving images. Or, students near the back may be less inhibited from chatting or texting, with each finger tap making the sound of an electronic water drop. One solution to avoid these distractions is to sit closer to the front of the room.

Another way to help focus your attention during class is to do the assigned reading before going to class, and as we indicated earlier, attempting to answer prequestions. Prequestions signal important information, and this information is typically relevant to your class lectures and assessments. The straightforward advice on using prequestions is to answer them before you read or attend class. Reading the material and answering prequestions helps to prepare you for the topics and content that will be presented. It will be easier to focus your thoughts on the key topics if you have thought about them previously than if you show up to class not having thought about them. Imagine walking into a movie without knowing anything about it, not even the title or actors. It takes you a while to catch up to speed with the movie. By reading in advance, it can also help you identify questions you may have about the content. As the lecture unfolds, your questions may be answered. If not, you could ask questions during class, during a break, or potentially at another time. The point is that having some awareness of the content in advance can make it easier to focus your attention during lecture.

If your instructor does not provide prequestions, ask the instructor if it is possible to provide some prequestions for assigned readings or for class to help you focus when you study. Here is a caveat: If you answer prequestions before you read, and then you merely search for answers in the text without actually reading, you run the risk of missing other information that will contribute to your understanding. For instance, suppose a question asks, "What is the primary function of the arteries in the circulatory system?" You may be able to find the answer to this question stated in one or two sentences (i.e., to distribute oxygen-rich blood away from the heart to the body). However, this information may be difficult to remember in the presence of other related facts (e.g., the veins distribute oxygen-depleted blood from the body to the heart), you may not recall the structure of the arteries (i.e., thick and elastic), or you may not understand how structure is related to function (i.e., thickness and elasticity enable the arteries to adjust to changes in blood pressure). Thus, prequestions should be answered to help you identify and think about particularly relevant information, not merely as criteria for locating isolated facts.

Further, you need to be able to adjust your study strategies based on how you are assessed in your classes. Your instructor may assign readings but only assess content from class notes. It can be difficult to motivate yourself to answer prequestions if they do not align with content that is targeted in course assessments. Nonetheless, instructors generally assign readings that are meant to help you develop a better understanding of a topic. Further, instructors may expect you to learn some content outside of class time, particularly information that is easier to understand. Instructors may do this so that there is more time in class to cover content that is more difficult to learn.

Using Knowledge of Attention: Teacher Perspective

We've discussed several things that can grab students' attention. The first was the **novelty** of the information. Novelty can be used to gain and maintain attention. Effective preschool teachers particularly understand the powerful influence of novelty. When parents drop off their kids at preschool, many of the materials and objects in the room differ each day. For example, they may put puzzles on the table on one day and playdough the next day. Or there may be different books, sports equipment, blocks, or toys, such as a train set, in the room. When kids arrive at preschool, their attention often shifts from their parents to these different materials and they become engrossed in exploring, which facilitates their cognitive development and ensures a clean escape for parents!

Emotional content also grabs attention. In the classroom, teachers can make lessons scary, funny, exciting, or contentious, with a great effect on attention. An elementary school teacher might assign books that are exciting, hilarious, or scary. Such emotional characteristics could serve to focus students' attention on a book. Knowing that some political topics can be emotionally charged, a high school or middle school teacher might ask students to take a stance on current debates for a research paper. The emotions that some students have about those topics could make it easier for them to focus on the assignment.

The physical properties of learning material can also attract attention. Contrast can be used when information is presented visually. **Bold**, *italicized*, and <u>underlined</u> words in a text contrast with words that lack these features. Changes in font size and indentation also stand out. Writers and textbook editors understand this and use contrast to help guide readers' attention to important information. An elementary English teacher, for example, could use different colors of marker to diagram sentences, using blue to signal the noun and red to signal the verb. These colors contrast with each other and differ from the other words in the sentence.

Teachers can also use contrast with their voices. For example, which person would be easier for you to pay attention to, someone who reads from a script or someone with voice inflection? It is difficult to pay attention to someone who is monotone. Someone who changes the pitch and volume of his/her words is much easier to pay attention to. Changing the speed of speech and incorporating dramatic pauses into speech can gain attention. For instance, upon hearing their teacher suddenly change her voice to a low, slow, urgent tone, students might think, "This must be important. I bet it's on the next test."

Movement can be utilized in different ways in a classroom. Teachers who move around the room while they give instructions or deliver a lecture, for example, are more likely to keep students' attention. Teachers can physically direct students' attention to relevant information on the board, such as a key term or a specific step in a math problem, by pointing to it or circling it with a laser pointer. A high school teacher who uses PowerPoint presentations to help guide students' note taking can incorporate "fly-in" bullet points when transitioning from one topic to the next.

One of the most important things to consider is to increase the relevance of the material for the student. Making a lesson relevant to students can help teachers gain and maintain students' attention. For example, consider a high school business teacher who is planning to teach students about the mathematical formula for computing compound interest. Students may struggle to pay attention to such an abstract concept. However, knowing her students will be driving soon, and that many of them will want to buy a car, she could begin the lesson by asking how much it costs to pay for a car if you get a $5,000 loan and then state that there is a way to save money when you apply a particular formula. It will be easier to gain and maintain the students' attention if owning a car is relevant to them.

Similarly, giving students task-orienting instructions, such as study questions, to accompany assigned readings, class lectures, or online videos can help them focus their attention on information that is relevant to the task. Prequestions can help students identify relevant information to study and to use their study time more effectively. One approach is to direct students to prequestions in their textbooks and encourage them to answer the questions before they read. Then, students could again answer the questions after they read. This can help students monitor changes in their learning and identify information that may need further study. Some online platforms have this function available with associated textbooks. Alternatively, you as an instructor can develop items that help students focus on what you believe is relevant or important to students.

Another approach is to include prequestions at the start of or during class. Later, you could revisit these questions in class. Students could answer the questions individually or in small groups, and then you could discuss the answers and provide feedback as a class. Or, you could send feedback to students electronically after class. A final word is that you need to consider students' perceived benefits of answering prequestions. Do you assess content that is targeted by prequestions? Are students rewarded for their efforts? This means that you need to consider whether it is necessary to provide credit for completion of assessment tasks that include prequestions and whether such content will appear on large assessment items.

Students are busy. As a teacher, it is important to keep in mind that students typically take multiple courses during the same term and have numerous readings for each course. Further, they often have responsibilities outside of being a student. If they are asked to spend time on a task in which they do not see the direct benefit, they will focus their energies on tasks that do. On the flip side, if you only assess items that pertain to the prequestions, students may opt not to read, and only attempt to identify and memorize the answers to the questions. And so, careful attention must be paid to how prequestions are used in a classroom.

Ensuring Students Avoid Attending to Distracting Information

You can use your knowledge of attention to ensure that students pay attention to information that will help them learn. However, you can also use your knowledge of attention to ensure that students avoid attending to information that can distract them from learning. Sounds coming into a classroom through an opened door, for example, can capture the attention of nearby students and away from their work.

Student teachers and other college students in field placements often believe their presence in the classroom is a disruption to students. This is probably true, but only until the novelty or unexpectedness of their presence wears off. For the same reason, a student with a physical disability, such as a student who uses an electric wheelchair, might initially be distracting to students in a classroom because of the novelty. Teachers can help reduce the novelty of a person's presence by quickly making that person's classroom participation commonplace. A teacher, in other words, should immediately begin interacting with students during class, and a student with a disability should immediately be included in all classroom activities. A middle school teacher could invite a new student with a disability, which slows his speech and body movement, to explain the nature of his condition to the class. This may immediately reduce the novelty of their new classmate.

Emotion is also an important consideration. Displays of emotion are nearly impossible for other students to ignore. Can you remember a time in school when a classmate became emotional and either started crying or giggling? If a student is crying, even quietly, it's a good bet that many other students notice and wonder why their classmate is upset. Dealing with a student who is upset or crying is never easy, but teachers need to realize that students' emotions can affect their attention and those around them.

Finally, just as movement can direct attention, movement can also be distracting. Students seated near a classroom window might have their attention drawn outside the window, where other students are playing kickball at recess or physical eduation. These students may struggle to focus on the teacher, a book, or an assignment. Teachers need to be mindful of such distractions, and eliminate them by keeping classroom doors closed when appropriate, or by closing window blinds at strategic times, such as when students are playing outside near classroom windows.

In sum, there are many potential distractions in a classroom. Keeping those to a minimum, and using techniques to draw students' attention to relevant information are basic starting points to then using the techniques and strategies to improve memory and comprehension that we discuss in the following two chapters.

ATTENTION AND PREPARING TO LEARN: SUMMARY OF KEY IDEAS

1. Attention is our ability to focus on specific stimuli or events for further processing.
2. Attention has a limited capacity (limited capacity assumption); we can only focus on a limited amount of stimuli, ideas, or events at any given time.
3. People focus their attention on novel stimuli.
4. Emotional content gains attention.
5. The physical properties of a stimulus can capture attention.

6. Students' attention can be directed to relevant information using movement (e.g., pointing), contrast (e.g., **bold**, *italicized*, or underlined print), and color (e.g., using different colors to show parts of a math equation). People focus their attention on relevant stimuli.
    a. Providing students task-orienting instructions, study guides, or prequestions can help them focus their attention and learn relevant information.
7. Given the limited capacity of attention, to promote learning, you must ensure that students pay attention to information that helps them learn, and avoid attending to information that distracts them from learning.
8. Distractions should be removed as much as possible from a study environment (for the student) or from a classroom environment (for the teacher).
9. Students should consider using study guides and/or prequestions before and after a lecture to help them identify and study particularly relevant information, not merely as criteria for locating isolated facts—it is important to read the material.

Improving Memory

Three

In this chapter, we discuss the benefits of having a time gap between study episodes (distributed practice) and the benefits of attempting to retrieve information from memory (retrieval practice), such as through self-testing. Specifically:

- study episodes are more beneficial when we take breaks in-between study episodes,
- attempting to retrieve information from memory is more beneficial than just re-reading,
- attempting to recall information is more beneficial than attempting to recognize information (e.g., multiple-choice test),
- a short delay (from minutes to a few days) between study and retrieval practice leads to higher rates of recall, and,
- two retrieval practice episodes is better than one, but only when there is a time gap between each episode.

Have you ever crammed for a test? Many students do. Perhaps they procrastinate, or perhaps they simply believe that it's the most effective way to study, particularly if the material is only tested one time. Of course, studying right before a test can be helpful for both learning and remembering information, for a short period. But cramming is not effective for long-term learning! Hopefully the objective is not just to remember the material for a day: our goal in education should be to promote learning and memory for long periods of time!

In this chapter, we discuss two key factors that influence the long-term durability of memory. The first key is **distributed practice**, which involves using a study schedule in which you spread out study episodes over time. When we study, it is beneficial if we study multiple times, and it is even more helpful if we take breaks in-between study episodes, or distribute our study episodes over time. For instance, separating study episodes by at least one day, rather than concentrating all of study into one session, is extremely useful for maximizing long-term retention. Although it may take longer to learn information when we distribute practice, the information is retained for much longer. Thus, the time interval that separates different study episodes of the same material affects our ability to retain information for longer periods of time.

The second key factor is **retrieval practice**, or practicing retrieving information from memory. Just as we have to practice to learn skills like riding a bike, practice is key to improving memory. Testing your memory is practicing your memory, and it has a powerful effect on learning. If you test yourself on information that you have previously learned, you are more likely to recall this information in the future than if you had not attempted to recall the information. Testing your ability to recall information not only allows you to assess whether you have learned something, it actually strengthens your learning.

DISTRIBUTED PRACTICE

People learn better when they spread their study across multiple periods of time rather than cramming. This is called the **distributed practice effect** (also known as the *spacing effect*). Distributing study over time is more effective (in the long run) than when study is clustered closely together in time. To understand why distributed practice is beneficial, think back to the ideas presented in Figure 1.1 in Chapter 1 (shown again below) about the three basic levels of information activation. When we initially encounter information and it is in our focus of attention, it is activated in memory. As time passes between study episodes, the information loses activation. However, when we restudy the information after a break, the information regains activation. This cycle of activation-deactivation-reactivation is beneficial for memory because it strengthens neural pathways in our brains, which increase our access to the information at later times.

In this chapter, we focus on improving learning and memory by retrieving information from long-term memory. When we learn information, it is in our focus of attention. But as time passes, the information loses activation. Repeated

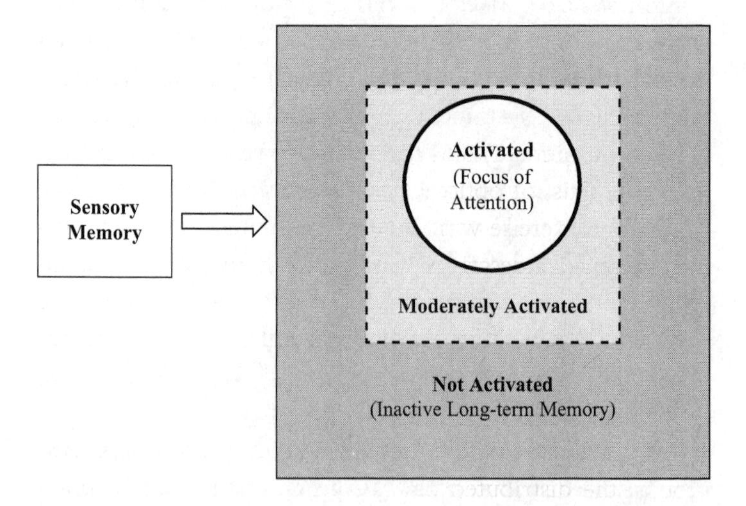

Figure 1.1 Three basic levels of information activation in human cognition

attempts to retrieve that information strengthens critical pathways to the information and improves learning and memory.

Retention Is Better When There Is a Time Gap Between Study Episodes!

It is more beneficial to have breaks in-*between study episodes* than to cram. Let's look at two examples to illustrate. The first example involves a 1-day interval between study episodes and the second example involves a several minute interval between study episodes.

An experiment by Kristine Bloom and Thomas Shuell[9] illustrates the idea that a 1-day interval between study episodes is more beneficial than back-to-back study episodes within a single day. Students in a high school French class were asked to learn 20 French vocabulary words and their English equivalents, a familiar task that was part of their regular classroom activities. In this instance, all of the words were the names of occupations (e.g., *l'avocat*, "lawyer"). The students completed a series of three 10-minute written exercises that were designed to help them learn the information. The first exercise was a multiple-choice test in which students received the English name (e.g., fireman) and had to identify the French equivalent from a list of options (e.g., *le proviseur, le facteur, le pompier*). The second exercise was a fill-in the blank test in which students received a description of the occupation in French and had to generate the name of the occupation in French. For the third exercise, students received the name of each occupation in English and had to write the French equivalent (e.g., businessman—__________).

The researchers randomly assigned students to one of two groups: the distributed practice group or the massed practice group. Students in the distributed practice group did one 10-minute exercise on each of three consecutive days (see

Table 3.1 Study design from Bloom and Shuell[9]

Group	*Day 1*	*Day 2*	*Day 3*	*4 Days later*
Massed practice group	Unrelated task	Unrelated task	30 minutes, then immediate test	Delayed test
Distributed practice group	10 minutes	10 minutes	10 minutes, then immediate test	Delayed test

Table 3.1). That is, they worked for 10 minutes a day, three days in a row. They were called the distributed practice group because they distributed their study time across three days. The second group was called the massed practice group. On Days 1 and 2 when the distributed practice group was completing exercises, they worked on unrelated French vocabulary tasks. On Day 3, they worked on the same three exercises as the distributed practice group, but did so for 30 consecutive minutes on a single day. So, both groups spent the same total amount of time (30 minutes) working on the same three exercises, but they distributed their study time differently.

On Day 3, immediately after students in both groups finished the last exercise, they were given a test (immediate test). Students received the name of each occupation in English and had to write the French equivalent, a task which was identical to the third exercise they had just completed. Four days later, without having the vocabulary list to study and without warning, students retook the test (delayed test). The results from the immediate test and the delayed test (retest) are shown in Figure 3.1.

As can be seen in Figure 3.1, performance on the initial test that was given immediately after study did not significantly differ for the two groups; the distributed practice group averaged about 84% correct responses, whereas the massed practice

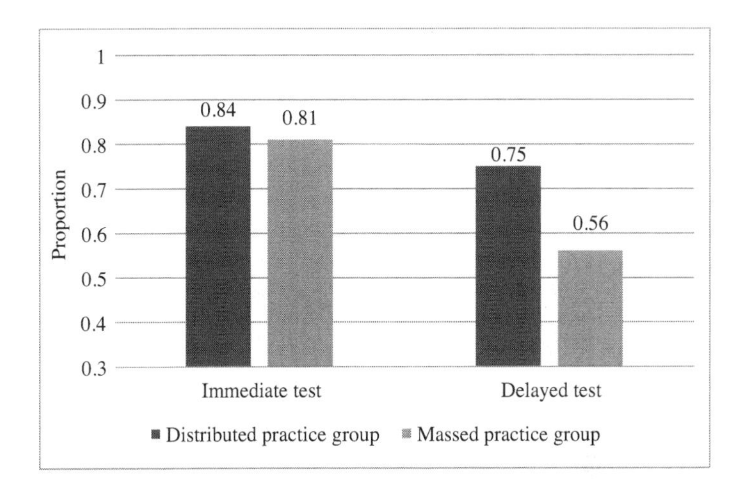

Figure 3.1 The results from Bloom and Shuell[9] show that a one-day interval between study episodes is more beneficial than back-to-back study episodes on the same day for long-term retention of information. (*The results are presented in terms of the proportion of items correct out of 20*)

group averaged about 81% correct responses. However, on the delayed test that was given four days later, students in the distributed practice group significantly outperformed students in the massed practice group; the distributed practice group averaged about 75% correct responses, whereas the massed practice group averaged about 56% correct responses. Although both groups showed a drop in performance, the students in the massed practice groups showed a much larger drop.

This study illustrates the point that an interval of at least 1 day between study episodes is more beneficial than studying within a single day, particularly for long-term retention.

However, even when a person studies within a single day, an interval of several minutes between study episodes is more beneficial than no interval between study episodes, such as when a person re-reads a definition multiple times in a row but does not revisit the information at a later time. An experiment by Frank Dempster[10] (Experiment 3) showed that a several minute interval between study episodes is more beneficial than having no interval between study episodes. Undergraduates were asked to learn 37 vocabulary words in either one of two groups. Each word and definition appeared on one page of a booklet (e.g., *loggia*—balcony), similar to when a student studies with flashcards. In the massed group, each word appeared three times in succession, whereas in the spaced group, there were 37 pages between each appearance of a word. Thus, the gap between words in the massed group was 0, whereas in the spaced group it was 37 (i.e., each appearance of a word was separated by 37 other words; which was just over 4 minutes). After doing a brief, 1-minute task that was unrelated to the words, students were given a list of the vocabulary words and asked to define them. The students in the spaced group outperformed the students in the massed group. Specifically, students in the spaced group recalled approximately 60% of the definitions, whereas students in the massed group only recalled approximately 36% of the definitions. Thus, if a person does not use at least a 1 day interval between study episodes, a brief interval (e.g., 4 minutes) between study episodes is better than no interval at all, at least for short-term retention (e.g., 1 minute).

As can be seen in the previous two studies, time gaps between study episodes can affect learning. In Bloom and Shuell's study[9], separating study episodes by one day led to better learning after a four-day delay. In Dempter's study[10], separating study episodes by approximately 4 minutes led to better learning than no interval between study episodes after a 1 minute delay. Thus, the time interval between study episodes affects learning, such that it is more beneficial to have breaks in-between study episodes of the same information, or to *distribute* our study episodes over time.

The Distributed Practice Effect Is More Pronounced When There Is a Time Gap Between the Last Study Episode and the Final Test!

The distributed practice effect is also affected by a second key variable: the amount of time *between the last study episode and the final test*. In general, the beneficial effect of distributed practice is more pronounced when the final test is given at least one month after the last study episode. This doesn't mean that you should stop studying a month before an exam! This means that if one person uses massed practice and another person uses distributed practice, when the final test occurs one month after the last study episode, the difference between individuals who use distributed practice and massed practice is amplified.

A study by Doug Rohrer and Kelli Taylor[11] (Experiment 1) illustrates the idea that the effect of distributed practice on learning is more pronounced 4 weeks after the final study episode than 1 week after the final study episode. These researchers investigated the effects of type of practice (massed vs. distributed) and the time between the last study episode and the final test (1 week vs. 4 weeks) on long-term learning (see Table 3.2). All students attempted to solve 10 math problems. Students in the distributed practice group solved 5 problems, and a week later solved 5 more problems. Students in the massed group solved all 10 problems in one session. Then, half of the students in both groups took a test either 1 week later or 4 weeks later.

Interestingly, when the test delay was one week, the average score for students in the distributed (70%) and massed (75%) practice groups were similar (see Figure 3.2). However,

Table 3.2 Study design from Rohrer and Taylor[11] (Experiment 1)

Group	*Session 1*	*Session 2 (1 week later)*	*Test delay after Session 2*
Distributed practice, 1 week test delay	5 problems	5 problems	1 week later
Massed practice, 1 week test delay	–	10 problems	1 week later
Distributed practice, 4 week test delay	5 problems	5 problems	4 weeks later
Massed practice, 4 week test delay	–	10 problems	4 weeks later

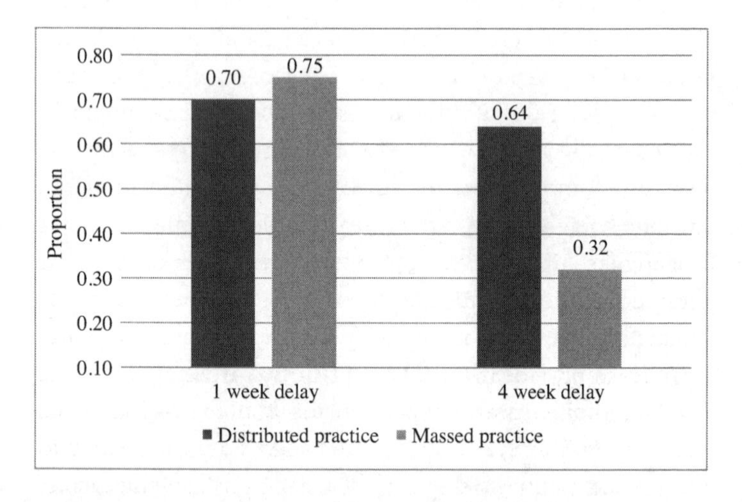

Figure 3.2 The results from Rohrer and Taylor[11] (Experiment 1) show that when the delay between the final study episode and the final test is longer (i.e., four weeks compared to one week), the benefit of distributed practice is more evident. (*The results are presented in terms of the proportion of items correct out of 10*)

when the test delay was four weeks, the average score for the students in the distributed group (64%) was double the score of the students in the massed group (32%). Thus, the benefits of distributed practice are more evident over the long term. So, for example, on a final exam, you're more likely to remember the information learned at the beginning of the semester if you have distributed your study episodes.

Notably, the majority of research on distributed practice pertains to vocabulary learning. This is generally the case because of measurement reasons (i.e., it is easy to measure isolated pieces of information and to control for study time). However, there is some research that shows a distributed practice effect for more complex forms of learning. The study by Rohrer and Taylor,[11] in which students solved math problems, is one example. Another example is a study by Nate Kornell and Robert Bjork[12] (Experiment 1A) who wanted to know whether the type of practice affected participants' ability to learn the painting styles of relatively unknown artists. This involves the process of induction, which is crucial skill involved in concept learning. Specifically, induction involves identifying similarities across related examples. For instance, seeing pictures of different types of dogs can enable individuals to distinguish dogs from cats or other mammals.

Kornell and Bjork wondered whether it would be more effective to provide massed presentation of artists' work rather than distributed presentation. On the one hand, distributed practice has a long history of enhancing learning relative to massed practice. However, on the other hand, massing makes it easier for a person to see the similarities across multiple paintings. Distributing the presentation may make it more difficult to infer a given artist's style.

All participants viewed six landscape paintings each from 12 different artists (i.e., 72 total paintings). In the massed practice condition, the paintings by each of the artists were presented consecutively, whereas in the distributed practice condition, the paintings by each artist were intermingled with paintings by other artists. In the testing phase of the study, which took place after a brief distracter task, participants were presented with new, previously unseen paintings from each of the artists. They were given a list of names of the artists and asked to indicate who had painted the picture. What were the results? The data showed that participants in the massed practice group correctly identified the artist of the picture approximately 35% of the time. In contrast, participants in the distributed practice group correctly identified the artist of the picture approximately 61% of the time, almost double the amount of the massed practice group! Thus, this study shows that distributed practice is effective for more complex forms of learning and further highlights the idea that time gaps between study episodes is beneficial for learning.

Using Distributed Practice: Student Perspective

As a student, attempt to use the following ideas to maximize the benefits of distributed practice.

First, study throughout the duration of a course, not just before quizzes, tests, and exams because spreading your study across multiple study episodes supports long-term learning. That is, you should spread your study time across the entire term rather than waiting for formal assessment from your instructor. This is actually easier than it sounds if you organize a schedule early in the term. This will help you establish a routine and learning will seem less daunting as the term unfolds. The largest predictor of new learning is past learning. So, if you spend time studying early in the term, you will reap the benefits later because you will continually strengthen your understanding over the term. Imagine only spending a few hours studying for final exams in the last week of the term rather than having stressful and inefficient cram sessions? Not only will life be less stressful, you are more likely to retain the information over the long term.

This means you need to set up and follow a regular study schedule throughout the duration of a course. There are numerous ways to do this from a time management perspective, so you need to decide how you slot in time to study. Whatever approach you take, it is important to schedule regular 'appointments' to study and not miss or cancel these appointments. You need to make sure that your academic and learning goals are reflected in how you spend your time, such that you should spend time on tasks that can contribute to these goals. You can study and still have a balanced life that includes social activities, exercise, chores, leisure, family responsibilities, and potentially a job. Doing this requires planning, identifying times that you can study, and sticking to your schedule.

Second, include time gaps between your study episodes. In particular, separating study episodes by at least 1 day, rather than concentrating all study into one session, is extremely useful for maximizing long-term retention. If you are unable to separate study episodes by at least 1 day, then separate study episodes by several minutes or hours. You may find it beneficial to take study breaks so that you can accomplish other tasks or goals, such as doing laundry, going to the gym, or meeting up with friends. These breaks can be beneficial, particularly when you stick to your study schedule.

Using Distributed Practice: Teacher Perspective

As a teacher, attempt to use the following practices in order to maximize the benefits of distributed practice.

First, administer frequent quizzes. Quizzes encourage students to distribute their study over the duration of a course because they know they are expected to study course content. Keep in mind that some assessments can be lower stakes in preparation for higher-stakes assessments. Similarly, administering frequent quizzes does not necessarily mean that quizzes need to be incorporated into course grades. For instance, students could complete a non-graded quiz about course content at the start of class and receive whole-class feedback about the correct responses at the end of class.

Second, revisit previously covered material. This can be done as a classroom activity. For instance, a teacher could periodically devote half of a class meeting to review information covered in the previous weeks. This could be a Jeopardy-style game in which the teacher poses questions, students generate responses, and the teacher provides feedback. This can also be incorporated into assessment tasks through the use of cumulative quizzes, tests, exams, or homework assignments. That is, give assessments throughout the course that include content that has been covered previously. On a quiz, for example, include several items from previous units. For homework assignments, students could receive a few problems or questions that pertain to information covered earlier in the school year. Cumulative assessments encourage students to study course material at multiple times during the course, not just content related to the current unit being studied.

It is important to note that although distributed practice is beneficial, it is unlikely that students will be able to remember everything throughout the school year. In fact, teachers may discover that students struggle to remember information that they could remember several weeks earlier. Distributed practice is not a panacea; nonetheless, students remember information better when they use distributed practice compared to when they don't use it. Further, even when students struggle to recall previously learned material, re-learning through review occurs more easily than the original learning. Thus, teachers can use distributed practice to strengthen memory following initial learning.

RETRIEVAL PRACTICE

Let's say that you have an exam coming up. Which would you do?

a. Read the material two times, or
b. Read the material and then try to recall it.

Most people choose letter *a*. But the better answer is *b*!

Retrieving Information From Memory Is Beneficial for Learning!

After you learn something, it is better to practice recalling the information than to re-read the information. That is, attempting to retrieve information from memory is more beneficial that just re-reading. This is called the **retrieval practice effect** (also known as the testing effect).

People generally assume that study time should be spent re-reading or reviewing information. It is common for students to believe that repeatedly reading or writing information leads to memory for that information. Hence, many students re-read their text or notes from class, or rewrite information during study. Students tend to focus their efforts on repeated exposure to information rather than self-testing. Further, in educational settings, instructional activities often involve the use of lectures, note-taking, reading, and so on.

While many of these practices may contribute to learning, a glaring omission is the role that testing can play in learning. Indeed, taking a test on information is usually viewed as a means to assess what we've learned, rather than a means to learn information. But, there is a good deal of evidence showing that *retrieval practice improves learning and long-term retention.* Retrieval practice is the act of attempting to activate information from memory, such as through testing or attempting to recall information.

Like distributed practice, to understand why retrieval practice is beneficial, think back to the ideas presented in Chapter 1 in Figure 1.1 about the three basic levels of information activation. When we initially encounter information and it is in our focus of attention, it is activated in working memory. As time passes between study episodes, the information loses activation. When we attempt to retrieve information in memory at a later time, the process of reactivation involves accessing related cues that point us in the right direction. Eventually, the information is re-activated. Repeated attempts to retrieve information strengthens the pathways to the information and speeds up the reactivation process.

An experiment by Roediger and Karpicke[13] (Experiment 2) provides a clear illustration of the influence of retrieval practice on memory. In Phase 1 of the experiment, university students were randomly assigned to one of three groups (see Table 3.3) and were asked to learn information from a short text passage (about 250 words). The first group was the repeated study group. These students studied the text during four consecutive study sessions that lasted 5 minutes each. The second condition was the single test group. These students studied the text during three consecutive study sessions that lasted 5 minutes each, then they had one test session in which they were asked to recall as much of the text as possible.

Table 3.3 Study design in Roediger and Karpicke[13] (Experiment 2)

Group	*Session 1*	*Session 2*	*Session 3*	*Session 4*
Repeated study (study x 4)	Study text	Study text	Study text	Study text
Single test (study x 3, test x 1)	Study text	Study text	Study text	Recall text
Repeated test (study x 1, test x 3)	Study text	Recall text	Recall text	Recall text

Note: Between each session, the students solved multiplication problems for 2 minutes. After the fourth session, all students solved multiplication problems for 5 minutes. They solved multiplication problems to minimize the effect of immediate memory.

The third condition was the repeated test group. Students in this group studied the text during one study session for 5 minutes, then had three consecutive test sessions in which they were asked to recall as much of the text as possible. Lastly, after the final session in Phase 1, students in all three conditions solved multiplication problems for 5 minutes to minimize the effect of immediate memory. That is, it is easier to remember material that is still in working memory—but recalling information that you are not thinking about is more relevant to learning.

In Phase 2 of the experiment, all students were tested on the information in the text. They were asked to recall as much information from the text as possible. However, students completed Phase 2 at different times. Specifically, half of the students took the test immediately after Phase 1 (i.e., after they had solved multiplication problems for 5 minutes) and the other half took the test one week after Phase 1. Thus, students only took the final test once; either an immediate test or a delayed test.

Which group had the highest score? It depends on whether the test was taken 5 minutes or 1 week after the final session (see Figure 3.3). When the test was immediate, the repeated study group (83%) recalled more than the single test group (78%), who in turn recalled more than the repeated test group (71%). However, when the test was delayed by 1 week, the order was flipped; the repeated test group (61%) recalled more than the single test group (56%), who in turn recalled more than the repeated study group (40%).

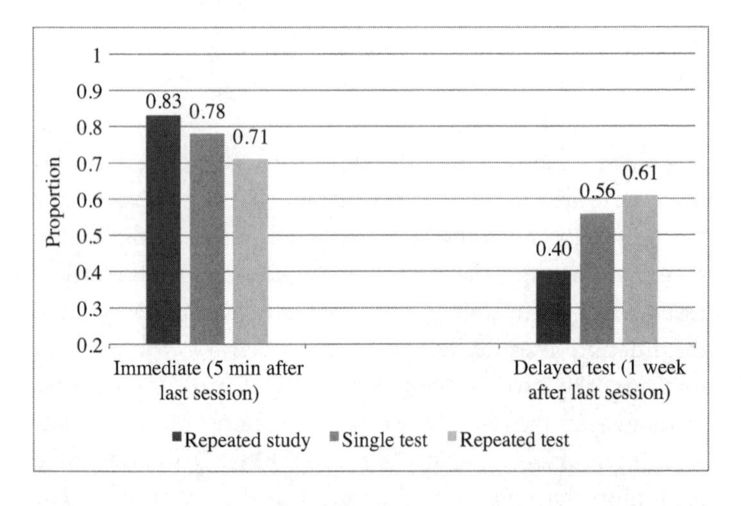

Figure 3.3 The results from Roediger and Karpicke[13] (Experiment 2) show that repeated study can lead to better memory for information at immediate test than (1) repeated study sessions and a single practice test, or (2) a single study session and three practice tests. However, after a 1-week delay, a single study session and three practice tests led to superior test performance. Testing as a study activity is beneficial for long-term retention of information. (*The results are presented in terms of the proportion of information ideas recalled out of 30*)

The experiment highlights several key ideas. When the test was immediate, repeated study led to the highest scores. This provides evidence that cramming can work in the short term, and perhaps explains why students commonly use this approach to studying. However, when the test was delayed by a 1-week gap, repeated testing was far superior to repeated study. This suggests that although additional study sometimes benefits learning in the short-term, testing during learning leads to better retention after a time delay. In sum, *retrieval practice is more effective than repeated studying for long-term learning.*

When Using Retrieval Practice, Attempting to Recall Is More Beneficial Than Attempting to Recognize!

Suppose you complete a reading for one of your classes at home and then you go to campus to meet up with a friend. Your friend sends a text that she will be 10 minutes late. To use your time productively, you try to remember everything from the reading you did for class without looking at the book. In that case, you are using what is called **free recall.** Free recall is a term used to describe attempts to retrieve information from memory without being given cues to help you retrieve the information. Conversely, recognition involves being given cues to help you retrieve information from memory. A multiple-choice test is an example of a recognition task in which you are given retrieval cues. For instance, if asked to define a key term on a multiple-choice test, you are given the correct answer among a range of distracters. Correctly responding requires recognizing the correct answer. Alternatively, a recall test would give you the term and you would have to generate the answer from memory. When studying, *attempting to recall information is more beneficial than attempting to recognize information.*

A study by John Glover[14] (Experiment 4a) illustrates the beneficial influence of retrieval practice via recall on memory. Students studied a short text passage (i.e., 300 words) on the fictitious nation of Mala. Glover wanted to investigate whether different types of retrieval practice would affect memory on a delayed test. So, he devised three different types of retrieval practice. The first type of retrieval practice involved free recall in which students were asked to recall as much of the text as possible. The second type of retrieval practice involved cued recall. For this task, students were given paraphrased sentence cues from the original text (e.g., Mala's form of government is _______) and were asked to fill-in the blank. The third type of retrieval practice involved recognition. For this task, students were given sentences from the short text and distracter sentences (i.e., related sentences that did not appear in the text), and were asked to indicate whether the sentence had appeared in the original text.

Essentially, the free recall is the most difficult of these three tasks because the fewest number of cues are provided to activate information in memory. And, cued recall is more difficult than recognition. So, Glover investigated whether the difficulty of the retrieval practice test would affect long-term memory. Students were randomly assigned to one of four groups which differed by the type of retrieval practice they used (see Table 3.4). Students in the *free recall group* studied the text, then 2 days later, did a free recall task for retrieval practice. Students in the *cued recall group* studied the text, then 2 days later, did a cued recall for retrieval practice. Students in the *recognition group* studied the text, then 2 days later, did a recognition test for retrieval practice. Students in the control group studied the text and did not do a retrieval practice test 2 days later. All students took a free recall test 4 days after they had initially studied the text.

Table 3.4 Study design in Glover[14] (Experiment 4a)

Group	*Day 1*	*Day 2*	*Day 3*	*Day 4*	*Day 5*
Free recall	Study	–	Free recall	–	Free recall
Cued recall	Study	–	Cued recall	–	Free recall
Recognition	Study	–	Recognition	–	Free recall
Control	Study	–	-	–	Free recall

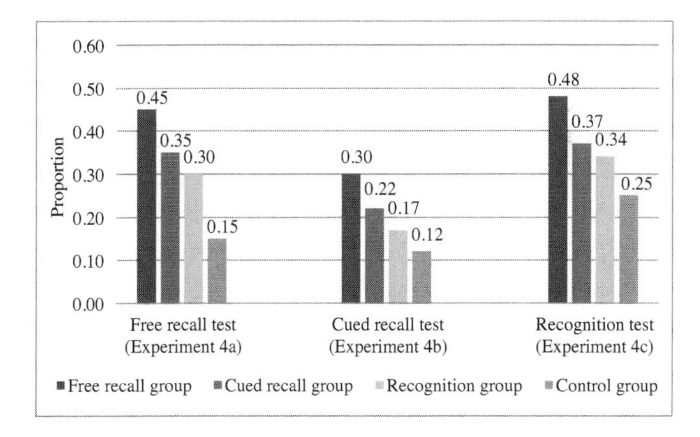

Figure 3.4 The results from Glover[14] (Experiments 4a, 4b, and 4c) show that free recall for retrieval practice is more beneficial than using cued recall or recognition for retrieval practice at delayed testing independently of the format of the posttest. (*The results are presented in terms of the proportion of information ideas recalled out of 24*)

What were the results on the final recall test on Day 5? The main finding was that students who used free recall for retrieval practice remembered more information than students in any other condition (see Figure 3.4, Experiment 4a). Thus, free recall for retrieval practice is more beneficial than using cued recall or recognition for retrieval practice.

Perhaps the students in the free recall group had an advantage over the other groups because the test on Day 3 was the same on Day 5. That is, the retrieval practice was identical to the final test, whereas the other students in the experimental groups did different tasks on Days 3 and 5. As it turns out, Glover addressed this by conducting two additional experiments. These were identical to the first experiment with one exception: the final test on Day 5 differed so that it matched the retrieval practice for one of the other groups. In one of the follow-up experiments, cued recall was used for the final test and in the other experiment recognition was used for the final test. If alignment between retrieval practice on Day 3 and final test on Day 5 is responsible for superior performance, then retrieval practice on Day 3 should be better when the final test matches the form of retrieval practice. That is, the cued recall group should have the best performance when the final test involves cued recall, whereas the recognition group should have the best performance when the final test involves recognition. Conversely, if free recall as a type of retrieval practice is more effective than cued recall or recognition, then the free recall group should have superior performance on the final test independently of the form of the final test. As can be seen in Figure 3.4, the data were consistent with the second explanation. The students who engaged in free recall for retrieval practice had higher scores than students in the other groups even when the final test matched the retrieval practice for the other groups. When the final test was cued recall (see Figure 3.4, Experiment 4b) and when it was recognition (see Figure 3.4, Experiment 4c), the free recall groups had the highest scores.

This indicates that free recall for retrieval practice is a **desirable difficulty**. A difficulty is considered to be desirable when the challenge involved in responding to a task supports learning. For example, a free recall for retrieval practice is more difficult than cued recall or recognition, but free recall as a form of retrieval practice supports long-term learning better than cued recall or recognition.

In Glover's experiments, there was a 2-day time gap between retrieval practice and the final test. Will these differences still occur when the time gap between retrieval practice and the final test is increased, such as a time gap of 1 month? A study by Butler and Roediger[15] provides evidence of the lasting influence of retrieval practice on long-term learning. In their study, undergraduates watched three video lectures on art history on consecutive days. Shortly after watching each video, students completed one of three study activities:

1. read a summary of the lecture,
2. take a multiple-choice test on the lecture, or
3. take a short-answer test on the lecture.

Thus, each student did all three study activities, but only one activity per video. For instance, if after the first video a student read a summary, s/he might take a multiple-choice test after the second video, and a short-answer test after the third video. Reading a summary of the lecture involves re-exposure to the content and is a re-study task. Taking a multiple-choice test involves recognition. Taking a short-answer test involves recall of information from memory. So, the short-answer test is the most challenging task because the student is given the fewest number of cues about the information.

Approximately 4 weeks after completing the study activities, students completed a final test on all three videos, a 90-item short-answer test. The results showed that the short-answer test was the most effective study activity to do after a lecture (see Figure 3.5). If students had done a short-answer test as a study activity, when they answered items on the final test about that content, they correctly answered 47% (14.1 out of 30) of the items. However, when students had done a multiple-choice test or read a summary as a study activity, when they answered items on the final test about that content, they only answered

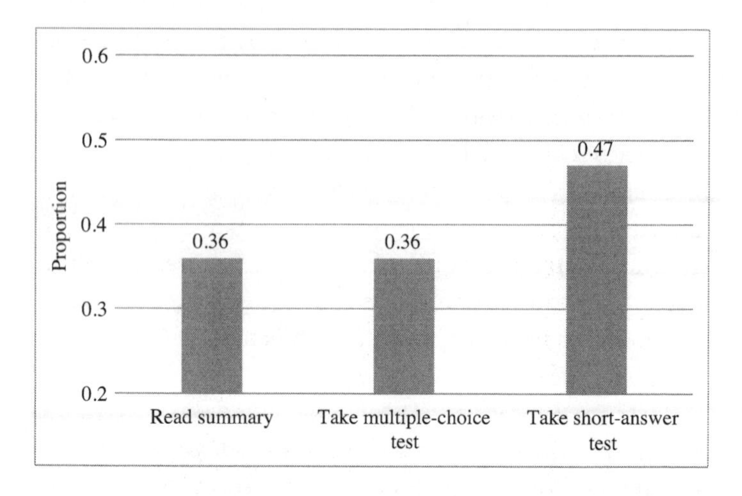

Figure 3.5 The results from Butler and Roediger[15] show that after a 4-week delay, cued recall (answering short-answer items) for retrieval practice is more beneficial than answering multiple-choice items for retrieval practice or reading a summary. (*The results are presented in terms of the proportion correct out of 30 for each study activity*)

36% of the items correctly (10.8 out of 30). That's a large difference, particularly given that there was a 4-week gap between the time in which they did each study activity and took the final test.

How Much Time Should Pass Between Initial Study and Retrieval Practice?

Attempting to retrieve information from memory is *not* beneficial if you ultimately are unable to recall the information. The best way to ensure that you will be able to recall information during a retrieval practice session is to minimize the amount of time between exposure to the information and retrieval practice. That is, a short delay between study and retrieval leads to higher rates of recall. However, this can present a problem for long-term learning. Retrieving information after a very short delay is somewhat similar to rote rehearsal, which leads to very low rates of recall on delayed measures of learning. It sounds like a Catch 22: the best way to ensure high rates of recall is to have a short delay between study and retrieval practice, but a short delay between study and retrieval practice does not lead to long-term learning. So what's the solution?

A study by Mary Pyc and Katherine Rawson[16] (Experiment 1) provides some insights into the time delay between study and retrieval practice. Students studied 70 foreign vocabulary terms for 10 seconds each and either had shorter time intervals of 1 minute between study and retrieval practice, or they had longer time intervals of 6 minutes between study and retrieval practice. In the shorter interval condition, students would attempt to recall a term 1 minute after they had initially studied it. In the longer interval condition, students would attempt to recall a term 6 minutes after they had initially studied it. Students in both conditions studied other terms during the time interval between initial study and retrieval practice. After students had studied all 70 terms, they completed a 25 minute reading comprehension task as a distracter task. Then, half of the students were tested on all 70 items immediately after the reading task and half were tested 1 week later (see Table 3.5).

Table 3.5 Study design from Pyc and Rawson[16] (Experiment 1)

Group	*Interval between study and retrieval practice*	*Time gap between final retrieval practice session and final test*
Shorter interval, shorter test delay	1 minute	25 minutes
Longer interval, shorter test delay	6 minutes	25 minutes
Shorter interval, longer test delay	1 minute	1 week
Longer interval, longer test delay	6 minutes	1 week

What did they find? As would be expected, the students who took the final test after a 25-minute delay did better than students who took the final test after a 1-week delay. This was to be expected because students generally do better when the final test occurs within minutes after studying compared to taking the test a week after studying. However, students who engaged in retrieval practice at 6-minute intervals scored higher than students who engaged in retrieval practice at 1-minute intervals, independently of when they took the final test. That is, when the final test was given *after a 25-minute delay*, performance was better after 6-minute retrieval practice intervals than after 1-minute intervals. Similarly, when the final test was given *after a 1-week delay*, performance was better after 6-minute retrieval practice intervals than after 1-minute intervals. Thus, these results suggest that a retrieval practice interval as short as 6 minutes is better than an interval of 1 minute, both when a final test occurs at a delay of half an hour or after a delay of 1 week (see Figure 3.6).

It is important to note that the data reported in Figure 3.6 was for students who studied each term and did retrieval practice once for each term. For simplicity's sake, we do not report the entire study. Nonetheless, the patterns were the same when students in other groups studied and attempted to retrieve numerous times.

Thus, Pyc and Rawson's research study[16] shows us that it is beneficial to have a time gap between study and retrieval practice. Specifically, they found that a gap of 6 minutes was better than a gap of 1 minute. But let's say you find it disruptive to your study routine to stop every 6 minutes to do retrieval practice and would rather do it after you are done reading or reviewing your notes. Is retrieval practice beneficial a couple of days after you initially study information?

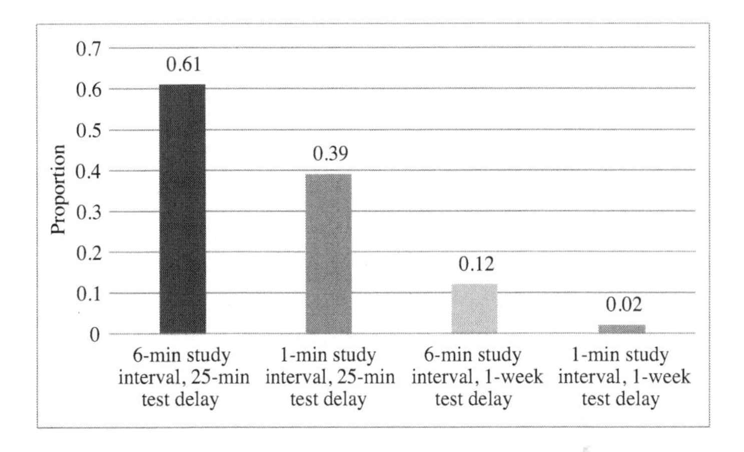

Figure 3.6 The results from Pyc and Rawson[16] (Experiment 1) show that a retrieval practice interval of 6 minutes leads to better performance than an interval of 1 minute, both when a final test is taken after a 25-minute delay or after a 1-week delay. (*The results are presented in terms of the proportion correct out of 70*)

Table 3.6 Study design in Glover[14] (Experiment 2)

Group	*Day 1*	*Day 2*	*Day 3*	*Day 4*	*Day 5*
Immediate retrieval practice	Study, Free recall	–	–	–	Free recall
Delayed retrieval practice	Study	–	Free recall	–	Free recall
Control	Study	–	–	–	Free recall

An experiment by Glover[14] (Experiment 2) suggests that time gaps as long as 2 days between retrieval practice sessions are beneficial. Undergraduates studied a short text passage. They were assigned to one of three groups (see Table 3.6). Students in the *immediate retrieval practice* group studied the text and then immediately did free recall retrieval practice. Students in the *delayed retrieval practice* group studied the text and then 2 days later did free recall retrieval practice. Students in the *control* group only studied the passage. Students in all three groups did a free recall test 4 days after they initially studied the passage.

The scores on the free recall test on Day 5 showed that students in the delayed retrieval practice group (45%) recalled substantially more information than students in the other groups, and scores for the students in the immediate retrieval practice (14%) and control (15%) groups did not differ (see Figure 3.7). Thus, retrieval practice after a 2-day delay was

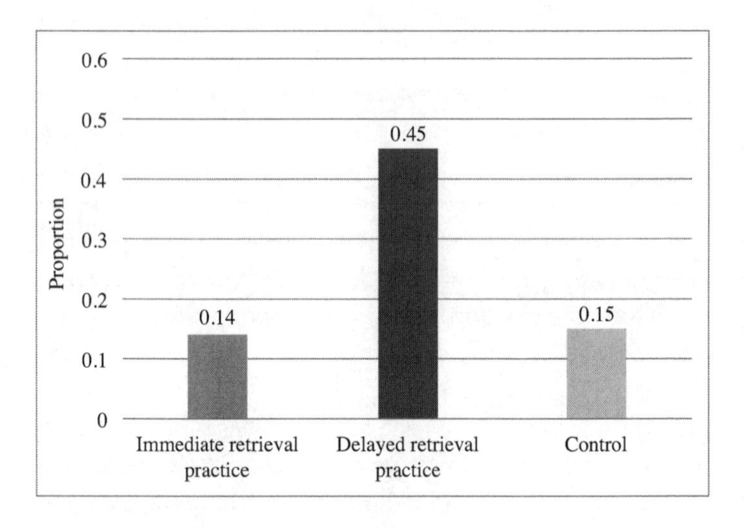

Figure 3.7 The results from Glover[14] (Experiment 2) show that retrieval practice after a 2-day delay is much more beneficial than retrieval practice immediately after study, and that retrieval practice immediately after study is no more beneficial than only studying when tested 4 days after the initial study session. (*The results are presented in terms of the proportion ideas recalled out of 24*)

much more beneficial than retrieval practice immediately after study. Further, immediate retrieval practice was no more beneficial than just studying the text passage. These findings suggest that immediate retrieval practice has limited or no benefit because the information is still available in working memory, whereas delayed retrieval practice is more beneficial because the information has to be accessed from long-term memory, and the act of retrieval enhances learning.

As has been shown, there is little or no long-term benefit to retrieval practice that occurs immediately after initial study (see Glover[14]; Experiment 2) or 1 minute after initial study (Pyc & Rawson[16]). But let's suppose that there is a longer time gap, such as 1 day, between initial study and retrieval practice. Further, suppose you want to use retrieval practice twice. Does it matter whether there are time gaps between your retrieval practice sessions? For instance, if you decide to use two retrieval practice sessions, beginning the day after your initial study session, does it matter whether your retrieval practice is massed or distributed?

Glover[14] (Experiment 3) investigated the role of retrieval practice with middle-school students who were learning about the parts of a flower. On the first day of the experiment, the students studied a drawing of a flower with 12 of the parts labeled (see Table 3.7). All students were given 15 minutes to study the drawing, and they were encouraged to draw their own version of the flower and to quiz themselves. On Day 2, students in the three experimental groups did retrieval practice; they received a drawing of the flower they had seen during the study session but none of the parts were labeled. Their task was to provide the labels from memory.

However, the amount and timing of the retrieval practice differed among the groups. Students in the *single* retrieval practice group did retrieval practice once on Day 2. Students in the

Table 3.7 Study design in Glover[14] (Experiment 3)

Group	*Day 1*	*Day 2*	*Day 3*	*Day 4*	*Day 5*
Single retrieval practice	Study	Free recall	–	–	Free recall
Massed retrieval practice	Study	Free recall, Free recall	–	–	Free recall
Distributed retrieval practice	Study	Free recall	Free recall	–	Free recall
Control	Study	-	–	–	Free recall

massed retrieval practice group did retrieval practice twice on Day 2, back-to-back. Students in the *distributed retrieval practice* group did retrieval practice once on Day 2 and again on Day 3. A control group only studied the information on Day 1 and did not do retrieval practice. Lastly, 4 days after the study session, students in all four groups completed a final test on the material. Again, students were asked to label the parts of the flower from memory.

The results are shown in Figure 3.8. There is a lot to think about with respect to this study. Let's focus on two particular elements individually and see what they tell us. First, we can see that retrieval practice after a 1-day delay is more beneficial than only studying the information. We know this because all three experimental groups did better on the final recall test than the control group. Second, two retrieval practice tests were more beneficial than one retrieval practice test, but only when the two retrieval practice tests were spaced apart. The distributed retrieval practice group did better than the massed retrieval practice group and the single retrieval practice group. Thus, distributing or spacing retrieval practice over time is more beneficial than massed retrieval practice. Further, there

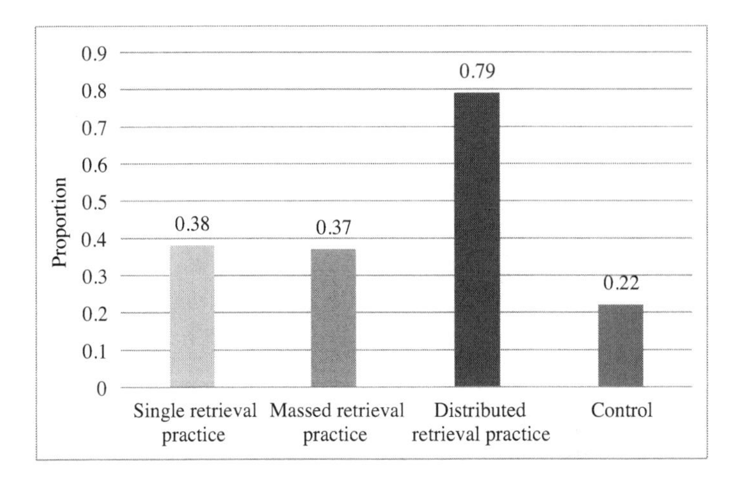

Figure 3.8 The results from Glover[14] (Experiment 3) show that retrieval practice after a 1-day delay is more beneficial than only studying information. More importantly, the results show that two retrieval practice tests are more beneficial than one retrieval practice test, but only when the two retrieval practice tests are spaced apart by 1 day. (*The results are presented in terms of the proportion of ideas recalled out of 12*)

is little or no benefit to massed retrieval practice after a 1-day delay compared to a single retrieval practice session. In sum, two retrieval practice episodes is better than one, but only when there is a time gap between each episode.

Using Retrieval Practice: Student Perspective

As a student, attempt to use the following activities to maximize the benefits of retrieval practice. For each activity, begin by selecting the most important information from your notes or readings. This ensures that your study efforts are directed towards appropriate information.

First, include retrieval practice in your study activities. Keep in mind that retrieving information from memory supports learning. Self-testing is one way to do this and there are several ways you can self-test. Flash-cards are easy to make and use. Look at a term and try to generate the definition, or vice versa; look at the definition and try to generate the term. Another approach is to use **key word** testing. Create an additional column in your notes, such as in the left-hand margin, that are used for key words. In the key word column, write key words that refer to important ideas in your notes. Then cover your notes so that you can only see the key word column. Attempt to retrieve and write down the correct ideas in your notes from memory. Or, let's say you need to read a chapter for one of your classes. Every 10 minutes, you could use retrieval practice to try to recall information that you had previously read. If you find this too disruptive, perhaps you could use retrieval practice when you are waiting in line at the grocery store or while commuting by bus (but not while driving!).

Second, when you self-test, use free recall. Attempt to recall information from memory rather than attempting to recognize information, such as answering multiple-choice questions. That said, answering multiple-choice questions when self-testing can be beneficial, and can be a viable option if your instructor or the book publisher provides you practice items. However, creating and answering effective multiple-choice items on your own often takes more time than attempting to recall information from memory.

Third, allow time to pass between initial study and retrieval attempts. That is, delayed retrieval practice is more beneficial than immediate retrieval practice. When time passes between initial study and retrieval attempts, it becomes more difficult to retrieve information. This is a desirable difficulty because the challenge involved in attempting recall of the information supports learning. A short time gap, such as 5 minutes may be beneficial, and longer time gaps, such as one day or more, may be beneficial. Regardless, retrieval practice will be more beneficial to you if there is a time gap between initial study and attempting to retrieve information from memory.

Lastly, allow time to pass between retrieval practice sessions. Distributed retrieval practice is more beneficial than massed retrieval practice. Thus, retrieval practice should occur after time has passed between initial study and retrieval attempts (see previous point), and there should be a time gap between retrieval attempts. So, for example, you could wait 1 day or several minutes between retrieval practice attempts.

Using Retrieval Practice: Teacher Perspective

As a teacher, attempt to use the following recommendations in order to maximize the benefits of retrieval practice. For each recommendation, begin by selecting the most important information that you expect students to know. This signals to students which information they should primarily direct their study efforts.

First, use practice tests as part of your regular class activities. Retrieving information from memory via practice tests supports learning. It increases students' ability to retrieve information, encourages them to study more often because they know they are accountable for the information, and can help students know what they need to spend more time studying because it helps them figure out what they do and do not know. Keep in mind that practice tests do not need to be graded or may be allocated a small portion of the total grade. This may reduce student anxiety associated with assessments.

One way to incorporate retrieval practice in the classroom is to use peer instruction. For this approach, you ask students to apply what they learned from readings or activities that they do before class. They answer questions or other forms of assessment that require the recall and application of ideas they have learned or encountered before class. At first, students answer the items on their own, then they work in groups to answer the questions and receive immediate feedback on whether their answer is correct.

Second, use recall tasks for practice tests. This could involve free recall tasks or cued recall tasks. For a free recall task, you could ask students to recall as much as they can about some topic that you have previously discussed. For a cued recall task, you could give students incomplete sentences and have them complete the sentences with key terms. If time constraints make free and cued recall tasks difficult to do, then give students several multiple-choice items. The main point is that you want students to practice retrieving information from memory.

Third, there should be a time delay between initial exposure to content and retrieval practice. This can be achieved in several ways. A teacher could begin class with a brief practice test that covers content from previously encountered content. Or, a teacher could have a brief break during class or at the end of class to review previously encountered content. The timing of these depends on the flow and length of the class. It is advisable to do a practice test at a natural break in the content or as you transition from one major topic to another so as not to disrupt the flow of class. Depending on the availability of technology and student familiarity with tools, students could complete practice tests at home via online tests. It is also important to provide feedback to explain why some answers are correct and other answers are incorrect. This can be done by providing and explaining the correct answer, and why other commonly selected answers are incorrect collectively to the group without singling out particular students. This encourages students to check their own work and to help them determine what information they need to spend more time studying.

Lastly, have time gaps between retrieval practice sessions. You may not have to time to do practice tests each day. But you should attempt to have them each week, if not more frequently. By having them once or more per week, it enables you to introduce time gaps between practice tests, and distributed retrieval practice is more beneficial for students than massed retrieval practice.

IMPROVING MEMORY: SUMMARY OF KEY IDEAS

Distributed Practice

1. Using a study schedule in which you spread out study episodes over time (distributed practice) is beneficial for long-term retention of information.
   a. Retention is better when there is a time gap between study episodes.
   b. Even when a person studies within a single day, an interval of several minutes between study episodes is more beneficial than no interval between study episodes.
   c. The distributed practice effect is more pronounced when there is a time gap between the last study episode and the final test.
   d. It is important to spread study across multiple study episodes and include time gaps between study episodes to support long-term learning.
2. Students should consider spreading their study across multiple study episodes to support long-term learning, including time gaps between their study episodes, and studying throughout the duration of a course, not just before formal assessments.
3. Teachers should consider administering frequent quizzes and revisiting previously covered material.

Retrieval Practice

1. Attempting to retrieve information from memory (retrieval practice) is beneficial for long-term learning.
   a. Retrieval practice is more effective than re-reading for long-term learning, but perhaps not for short-term retention.
   b. When using retrieval practice, attempting to recall is more beneficial than attempting to recognize. Attempting to recall information is a desirable difficulty.
   c. A short delay (from minutes to a few days) between study and retrieval practice leads to higher rates of recall.
   d. It is important that information is not available in working memory because retrieving the information from long-term memory strengthens the connections in long-term memory.
2. Students should consider including retrieval practice in their study activities, using free recall for retrieval practice, allowing time to pass between initial study and retrieval practice, and allowing time to pass between retrieval practice sessions.
3. Students should consider using distributed practice, and in particular, use retrieval practice during study episodes.
4. Teachers should consider using practice tests as part of their regular class activities, using recall tasks for practice tests if students have encountered the material or have at least a basic understanding of the content, having a time delay between initial exposure to content and retrieval practice, and including time gaps between retrieval practice sessions.

Improving Comprehension

Four

In this chapter, we discuss factors that impact comprehension of text and ways of improving comprehension, particularly when the text (or lecture) is challenging. Specifically, this chapter covers:

- factors that affect comprehension,
- the benefits of generating questions,
- the benefits of elaborating and explaining text, and
- the benefits of completing graphic organizers.

Thus far, in the previous two chapters, we have discussed several techniques to improve attention and memory. But, what if you don't understand the content? Sometimes we need to remember words, lists, items, definitions, and so on that (for the most part), we understand. However, much of the content that students need to understand in a lecture or textbook can be challenging. Let's consider a section from a biology text book in Box 4.1.

This text is challenging to understand on many levels. It contains challenging vocabulary, concepts (e.g., photosynthesis, glucose, carbon, atoms, dioxide), and formulae; it contains long, syntactically challenging sentences; there is little overlap between sentences in terms of words and

Box 4.1

Photosynthesis is the process by which plants use energy from the sun to make glucose as a means of storing the energy for later use. The source of carbon atoms for the sugar is carbon dioxide, and the overall reaction is $6CO2 + 12H \rightarrow C6H12O6 + 3O$. The earliest and most primitive photosynthetic bacteria used hydrogen sources such as H2S or even molecular hydrogen, H2, to reduce CO2 sugars. At an early stage of evolution, however, organisms invented the machinery to obtain hydrogen from water, the most abundant source.

concepts (it is low in cohesion); and there is no explicit link between the concepts and real world ideas that are more familiar to students.

The features of a text are important considerations. Text is easier to understand when it has more accessible vocabulary and simple sentences. Texts are often given **readability** or grade level ratings. These are based on estimates of the potential familiarity of the words to the reader and the syntactic complexity of the sentences. For example, the first sentence of the text in Box 4.1 would be estimated at a grade level of 11–12 (ages 16–18) by most common formulas. This is because it contains many uncommon words and it is a long sentence (25 words) with many clauses. This complex sentence could be rewritten as:

> Photosynthesis is how plants use energy from the sun. They need energy to make glucose. This helps plants to store energy for later use.

Without adding new words or explanations, this modification lowers the estimated grade level substantially (depending on the formula), and would potentially make the content easier to understand.

Readability, however, is only one factor to consider. Another is **cohesion**. A text is more cohesive when it includes overlapping words and concepts between sentences and paragraphs. Cohesion is particularly important when readers have less knowledge about the content. Unless you have a substantial amount of knowledge about science and in particular, chemistry, you might be a relatively low-knowledge reader for this passage. Low-knowledge readers are less able to fill in the gaps in the text and are less able to infer the relations between ideas in the text. For example, the excerpt in Box 4.1 contains almost no overlap in words between the sentences, and there is only one connective (however) that spells out any of the relations. So, understanding and then remembering the relations between the ideas would be very challenging for a low-knowledge reader.

Prior knowledge helps students to understand challenging text. If you do know a lot about biology and chemistry, the text in Box 4.1 might be fairly easy to comprehend. But for most readers, there are many unfamiliar terms, concepts, processes, and symbols. By contrast, narrative texts usually contain a greater amount of familiar concepts and have more connections to real-world experiences for the reader. But, unfamiliar information is common when students are learning new content from expository texts and textbooks. They can be better prepared to understand challenging text when they can use prior knowledge that they have acquired either through previous classes or previous experiences outside of school. But, doing so is not automatic.

Indeed, students are often faced with text that is challenging to understand. Many texts include unfamiliar words, complex sentences, or gaps in cohesion. What can students do in these situations? Models of reading comprehension can guide the answer to that question. Accordingly, reading is the process of interpreting and extracting meaningful information from text (and discourse) and linking that information to prior knowledge in long-term memory. Making connections! This complex process requires a number of cognitive abilities and language skills, including the ability to recognize and understand written words, as well as the ability to comprehend language at a deep level. Beyond the processing of the words, the reader must understand the sentences in a text, as well as the relationships among the sentences. Readers of all ages benefit from learning about reading strategies, knowing how to use them, and knowing when to use them to understand text.

In this chapter, we discuss three such strategies: generating questions, elaborating and explaining text, and completing graphic organizers. We discuss these strategies because they have been shown to be effective in improving students' understanding of challenging text across multiple age levels and multiple types of texts. A commonality among these three strategies is that they all involve actively generating information and they can easily act as a means for retrieval practice (see Chapter 3).

GENERATING QUESTIONS

In Chapter 2, we discussed the benefits of *answering* questions before reading a text or viewing a video presentation. Another related strategy is *generating* questions while reading. For example, let's consider the first sentence from Box 4.1. There are several questions that a reader might generate. For example:

1. What is photosynthesis?
2. What is glucose?

3. How is glucose created from the energy of the sun?
4. Why do plants need to store energy?

Notice that these questions vary from more shallow (but perhaps important) questions regarding the meaning of the words (photosynthesis, glucose) to deeper questions: the *how* and *why* questions. Shallow questions are potentially important if you don't know the vocabulary in a text. At the same time, the deeper questions are also important to ask because they help you build relations between the ideas (and sentences) in a text. Because those relations are not always stated explicitly, it is important that students infer them; and students need to learn how to generate inferences.

Generating High-Quality Questions Is Beneficial for Comprehension!

Generating questions before reading can help you activate prior knowledge from long-term memory and can also help you look for information that you do not understand. Generating questions during and after reading can help you monitor or assess your comprehension of the ideas included in a text. Equally important, it is beneficial to answer those questions. This can be done through **self-explanation** (described in the next section), by searching for the answer in the text, by asking the teacher or possibly informed classmates, or from other resources (e.g., search other documents). The modern world has made this process easier, because we can simply seek the answer on the Internet (although this also involves judging the credibility of the source).

There is a great deal of research evidence that students who ask good questions also recall more information from the text and answer more questions correctly about the text.[17] Further, when students learn how to generate questions, they ask better questions and their text comprehension improves.

A study by Ruth Cohen[18] illustrates the benefits of instruction and practice in generating questions. Cohen wanted to know whether it was possible to teach young students (8-year-olds) to generate questions while they read short stories and whether such training would affect reading comprehension. To do this, she had third-grade children complete two pretests. The first pretest was a question-generation test in which students read five short stories. For each story, they were asked to state what the story was about (1 point) and to generate two good questions for each story (up to 5 points for each question). The scoring criteria for the questions focused on features such as whether the questions could be answered with information from the story and whether it was about important information from the story. Thus, students could earn up to 11 points per passage, or maximum of 55 points across all five stories. The second pretest was a standardized reading comprehension test, which is commonly used to assess students' comprehension abilities. Then, students were assigned to one of two groups (see Table 4.1).

Students in the *question-training* group worked in their classrooms for ten 15–20 minute training sessions. These students were taught about what makes good questions and practiced writing questions (Part I), then they were taught how to apply these questioning skills while reading narrative short stories (Part II; see Table 4.2). Students in the *no training* group (i.e., control group) did not receive any training and simply continued their classwork while the experimental group received training. After the question-training group completed their training, students in both groups again completed a question-generation test and a standardized reading comprehension test.

Table 4.1 Study design from Cohen[18]

Group	*Pretest*	*Part I*	*Part II*	*Posttest*
Question generation group	Question-generation test Reading comprehension test	Training in question generation	Application of question skills	Question-generation test Reading comprehension test
No training group	Question-generation test Reading comprehension test	Regular classroom activities	Regular classroom activities	Question-generation test Reading comprehension test

Table 4.2 Question generation training in Cohen[18]

PART I: Training Question Generation
(15 min/day for 6 consecutive days)

1. What makes a question a question?
   a. Questions ask for an answer
   b. Questions end in a question mark
2. What makes a good question?
   a. Good questions start with a question word
   b. Good questions can be answered by the story
   c. Good questions ask about important details of the story
3. Practice generating good questions for paragraphs

PART II: Application of Question Skills
(20 min/day for 4 consecutive days)

1. Read a story to answer "What is the story about?"
2. Generate two good questions for the story
3. Read to answer the generated questions
4. Generate new questions if questions are poor

As can be seen in Figure 4.1, students in the question-training group improved substantially from pretest to posttest, whereas the no question-training group's scores did not change.

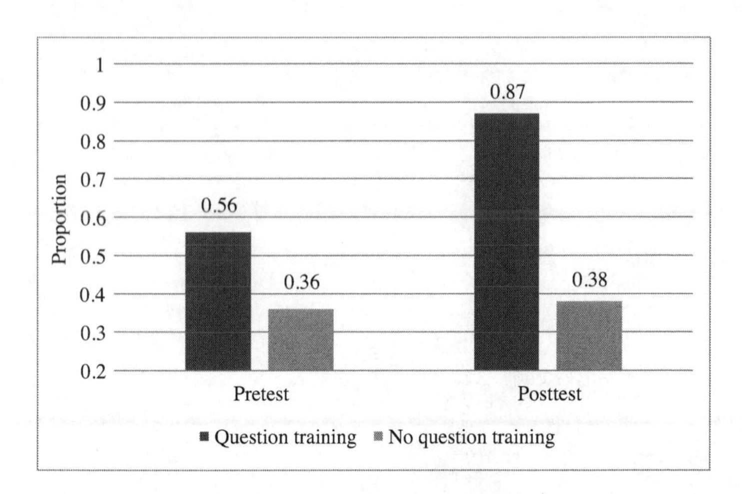

Figure 4.1 The results of Cohen[18] demonstrated that students as young as 8 years of age can be taught to generate questions while they read and that instruction in generating questions can improve the quality of the questions they generate. (*The results are presented in terms of the proportion of points received out of 55*)

Thus, these data showed that students as young as 8 years of age can be taught to generate questions.

Further, Cohen wanted to know whether training students to generate questions would enable them to spontaneously transfer these skills to the standardized reading comprehension test and improve their performance. What did the results show? As can be seen in Figure 4.2, the question-training group improved from pretest to posttest, whereas the no question-training group's scores did not change. Therefore, two conclusions can be drawn from this study. First, young children can be taught to generate questions while reading. Second, generating questions about a passage can enhance reading comprehension. Thus, receiving instruction in how to generate questions is beneficial for learning.

In Cohen's study, students engaged with narrative texts, for which students can rely on their knowledge of story

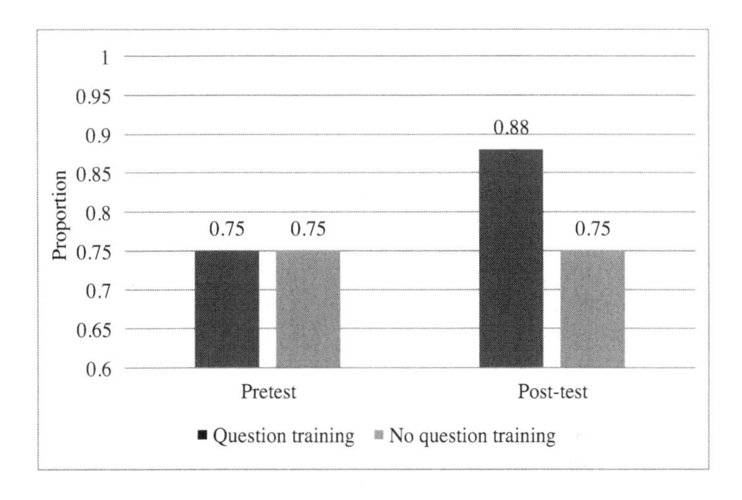

Figure 4.2 The results of Cohen[18] demonstrated that instruction in generating questions can improve performance on standardized reading comprehension test scores. (*The reading comprehension test was scored out of 8 points*)

structure (e.g., characters, events, conflict, resolution) to help them understand the text. A study by Beth Davy and Susan McBride[19] also demonstrated the benefits of teaching elementary students (approximately 10 years old) to generate questions but for expository texts, which are often informationally dense and contain unfamiliar terms and concepts, such as the example about photosynthesis at the beginning of this chapter. Students were assigned to one of five groups. Each group met for five 40-minute sessions over the course of 2 weeks, and engaged with three short expository texts (~240–280 words) during each session. The students in the *question-training* group were taught the following:

- Why question generation is beneficial
- How to generate *literal questions* (i.e., questions about explicitly stated information) and *inference questions* (i.e., questions

about implied ideas, or linking together information from different parts of the text)
- How to use signal words in question stems (following a *wh-* structure, such as what and why)
- How to formulate appropriate responses
- How to evaluate the quality of their questions

In the instructional sessions for the question-training group, the teacher introduced and demonstrated each skill; then students practiced the skill and received feedback.

The students in the other four groups either (1) were asked to generate questions but were not taught how to do so nor were they provided feedback, (2) responded to literal questions about the text, (3) responded to inference questions about the text, or (4) found definitions to underlined words in the text. After all students completed their respective training sessions, they read four texts that they had not previously seen and completed several tests. Further, they reported how well they thought they did on the question. The students in the question training group wrote higher quality questions, scored higher on both literal and inference comprehension questions, and provided more accurate predicts of their performance on the comprehension questions compared to the students in the other four conditions.

In sum, these two studies[18,19] and other similar studies[17] demonstrate the benefits of teaching students to generate questions. Specifically, it is beneficial for comprehension when students are taught (1) the importance of generating questions, (2) how to generate questions, (3) how to answer their own questions, and (4) how to evaluate the quality of their own questions. Teaching students about generating questions requires more than simply telling students to ask questions while reading. It is important for students to practice these strategies and to receive feedback on their performance. For younger students it may be more appropriate to practice with narrative texts, but for older students, it is beneficial to practice with expository texts that challenge their comprehension and require them to access and use their prior knowledge.

ELABORATING AND EXPLAINING TEXT

Another way to make connections between prior knowledge and new information is to explicitly elaborate on what the new information means—or to explain it. This is particularly useful and important when we know less about the topic. Suppose you are learning about the human circulatory system and are studying the difference between arteries and veins. While reviewing your class notes, you see that the arteries are more elastic and carry oxygen-rich blood away from the heart, whereas veins are less elastic and carry blood that is rich in carbon dioxide back to the heart. One approach to studying this information is to merely repeat the facts over and over, a strategy known as rote rehearsal. As we discussed in Chapter 3, this strategy is generally ineffective. Another approach is to clarify the significance or meaning of the facts in relation to each other; that is, to explain how ideas are related.

For instance, you could elaborate that it would make sense that the arteries are more elastic because they need to rapidly expand and contract to handle powerful bursts of blood when it is propelled away from the heart throughout the rest of the body. Similarly, you could elaborate that it would make sense that the veins are less elastic because they have less need to manage large changes in blood pressure. This second approach involves generating elaborations to explain the significance of to-be-learned information. This type of approach is more beneficial than rote rehearsal for learning declarative knowledge.

Generating Explanations Is Beneficial for Learning!

When you study, generating elaborations or **explanations** is beneficial for learning. Students commonly reread or rewrite information when they study if for no other reason than that they are unaware of other approaches to studying. While re-exposure to information can facilitate memory for immediate or short-term testing (e.g., cramming the night before a test), it is less effective than generating elaborations for long-term learning.

When Encoding Information, Making Information Meaningful Facilitates Memory!

One way to make information more meaningful is to generate elaborations. Generating an elaboration involves explaining the significance of to-be-learned information. Elaborations are effective because they provide cues to retrieve, and ultimately use, the information in the future. For this reason, elaboration is often a more effective process for encoding and retrieving large amounts of information than merely repeating given information or being given elaborations by someone else.

A study by Michael Pressley and several colleagues[20] (Experiment 1) illustrates the benefit of generating elaborations. University students were asked to read 24 sentences under one of three conditions. Students in the *no elaboration* group read sentences that did not include elaborations. For example, one sentence was, "The tall man bought the crackers." Students in the *self-generated* elaboration group received these same sentences; however, after they read each sentence they answered the following question, "Why did that particular man do that?" Students in the *given elaboration* group read the same sentences, but they read additional information that indicated the significance of the connection between the man and the action (e.g., The tall man bought the crackers that were on the top shelf).

There was another element to the study. The researchers also wanted to investigate whether it mattered if students knew they were going to be tested on their memory for the information. Perhaps students will approach the task differently if they know they'll be tested. So, half of the participants were told that the purpose of the experiment was to determine how easy certain sentences were to understand, and the other half of the participants were told the purpose of the experiment was to determine how well they could learn sentences. Thus, there were six groups in the study (see Table 4.3). For instance, the box with the details "no elaboration, ease of understanding" was one group who *read sentences without elaborations* and who were told that the purpose of the experiment was to *determine how easy certain sentences were to understand*.

After they read all of the sentences, all of the students completed a cued recall task. For the cued recall task, students

Table 4.3 Study design from Pressley and colleagues[20] (Experiment 1)

Type of elaboration	*Perceived purpose of the experiment*	
	Ease of understanding sentences	*Learn sentences*
No elaboration	No elaboration, ease of understanding	No elaboration, learn sentences
Self-generated elaboration	Self-generated elaboration, ease of understanding	Self-generated elaboration, learn sentences
Given elaboration	Given elaboration, ease of understanding	Given elaboration, learn sentences

received a "who" question that pertained to each of the 24 sentences that they had read earlier (e.g., Who bought the crackers?) and had to recall the type of man who had done the action in the sentence (e.g., The tall man).

What were the findings? Let's first focus on the groups that were told the purpose of the experiment was to determine how easy certain sentences were to understand. These students rated each sentence for comprehensibility (1 [*very easy to comprehend*] to 7 [*very difficult to comprehend*]) and were not expecting to be tested on the information. When students generated their own elaboration, it was no contest (see Figure 4.3). Their scores were over 4 times greater than the no elaboration group and 2.5 times greater than the given elaboration group. That is, students in the *self-generated elaboration* group correctly recalled the type of man who had done the action in the

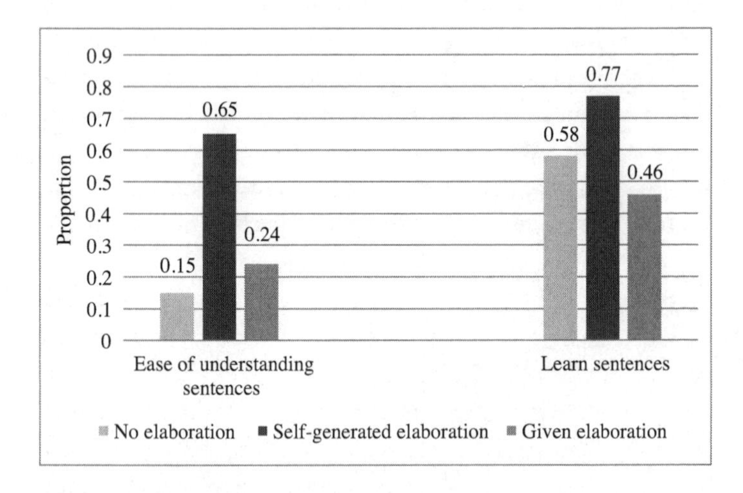

Figure 4.3 The results from Pressley and colleagues[20] (Experiment 1) show that students who were explicitly told to learn the sentences performed better overall, but the students who generated elaborations performed well regardless of which group they were in. (*The results are proportion of items correct out of 24*)

sentences significantly better than students from the other two conditions. Clearly, self-generated elaboration was superior to the other two approaches for remembering the information. However, these students were not expecting to be tested on the information. Would the results differ if students anticipated that they would be tested on the information? As can be seen in Figure 4.3, being asked to *learn sentences* made a difference for each group. When participants were told the purpose of the experiment was to determine how well they could learn sentences, students in all three groups showed better performance than students who did not expect to be tested. For instance, for the no elaboration group, scores were 58% for those who expected to be tested, but only 15% for those who did not expect to be tested.

However, two additional findings are particularly interesting. First, there is a clear benefit to self-generated elaborations. This was the most beneficial study activity independently of whether students expected to be tested. Second, when students expected to be tested on the material, it was more beneficial to try to remember the information in the sentence *without* a given elaboration. This indicates that some students may have generated elaborations on their own, particularly when the text was not already elaborated (and more cohesive).

One important aspect to the study conducted by Pressley and colleagues[20] is that the text was relatively familiar and thus the students could readily elaborate the text. However, textbooks oftentimes include information that is challenging and thus students lack sufficient prior knowledge to easily understand the content. In these cases, it may be difficult for these students to generate meaningful elaborations.

What can low-knowledge students do when faced with challenging text? Many students do not generate elaborations on their own, and if they do, their elaborations are not usually particularly high in quality. And, it is just these students who need to learn strategies to help them tackle challenging text. In response to this problem, McNamara[21] developed an intervention called **self-explanation reading training** (SERT) that combined instructions to self-explain text with instructions and practice using effective comprehension strategies (i.e., comprehension monitoring, paraphrasing, prediction, using logic and common sense, elaborating, and making bridging inferences; see Table 4.4).

Self-explanation is an explanation that is directed toward oneself, with the express purpose of constructing the meaning of the text. Explanations are statements, spoken aloud, written, or stated to oneself, that go beyond the text to explain the ideas, their relations, and their underlying meaning. However, like elaborations, many students do not generate high-quality, effective explanations. Combining self-explanation with instruction to use effective comprehension strategies affords opportunities to practice using the comprehension strategies. In turn, the quality of the self-explanations improve.

The six comprehension strategies included in SERT were ones that skilled readers use more often, and had been shown to improve students' comprehension with extensive practice[22]. The comprehension strategies are presented in SERT as a means to improve the self-explanation process. Comprehension monitoring is presented as a strategy that should be used all of the time. Paraphrasing is presented as a way to begin the process of self-explanation. The remaining strategies are various forms of inferences (i.e., domain specific, domain-general, predictive, and bridging) that typically enhance comprehension and explanation. Generating inferences creates links between ideas in the text and to prior knowledge, tying the ideas together like constructing a spider's web or a fisherman's net.

Table 4.4 Examples of comprehension strategies taught in Self-Explanation Reading Training (SERT) by McNamara[21] for the sentence: *Mitosis guarantees that all the genetic information in the nuclear DNA of the parent cell will go to each daughter cell*

Comprehension Strategy	*Examples*
Comprehension Monitoring: being aware of understanding	1. I don't remember what DNA stands for. 2. So I guess daughter cells are a part of a larger cell or came from a larger cell—I don't know.
Paraphrasing: restating the text in different words	1. So each daughter cell will receive a duplicate copy of the same strand of DNA from the parent cell. 2. Ok, through this process of mitosis all the genetic information belongs in the DNA of the parent cell and that is transferred over to the daughter cell.
Prediction: predicting what the text will say next	1. Ok, this is the separation of the cell—the DNA—the next one should be the RNA. 2. So, that's the first stage, now they'll give the second one.
Using Logic: using general knowledge and logic to understand the text (i.e., domain-general knowledge-based inferences)	1. Ok, what they're saying is that mitosis will make sure that an equal amounts of genetic information will go to each of the cells—equal amount will go to each daughter cell that way. They will develop basically the same—multiply the same. 2. Ok, so the genetic information that must be the chromosomes because the chromosomes are going into each of the cells. And that is made up of the DNA. So a part of . . . a part of each of the . . . a part of genetic information which is the DNA goes into each of the two cells that come out of this.

(Continued)

Table 4.4 (Continued)

Comprehension Strategy	*Examples*
Elaborating: using prior knowledge or experiences to understand the sentence	1. Ok, so there's the daughter cell and then there's a parent cell—mitosis it has to do with genetic information so when I'm thinking of cell division I'm thinking of maybe how a baby is made and how it's developing. 2. So, by mitosis it guarantees that the chromosomes will get passed on so that the traits or whatever will be able to live on or whatever.
Bridging: making reference to an idea presented in a previous sentence in the text to better understand relationships between sentences	1. So, mitosis—the first stage of cell division where each set of chromosomes goes to each daughter cell will contain DNA. 2. So, yeah, so all the genetic information is in the chromosomes and each cell gets a complete set, so that's mitosis—when each cell has just as much DNA as the first mother cell—main cell—parent cell.

McNamara[21] demonstrated that undergraduates who lack sufficient background knowledge particularly benefit from SERT. In her study, there were two groups. Students in the SERT group received reading strategy instruction and self-explanation practice with four texts, whereas students in the no training control group only read the four texts. After the training phase was done for the training group, students in both groups self-explained a difficult text about cell mitosis and answered comprehension questions about the text. The results showed that low-knowledge students who received self-explanation training had higher performance on literal questions about the text (51%) than students in the no training group (26%). Further, she found that using logic and making bridging inferences were crucial to enhancing low-knowledge students' understanding of the challenging text about cell mitosis. These were strategies that helped the students work through the text and essentially overcome their knowledge deficits by making use of world knowledge, logic, and common sense.

Next, let's consider a classroom study by McNamara[23] which demonstrates the benefits of a classroom intervention in self-explanation reading training (SERT) on course performance. The participants were first-year university students who were enrolled in an introductory biology course. Some of the students volunteered to receive SERT training, whereas others did not. Although they were not randomly assigned, the two groups of students were equivalent in terms of their reading ability, general knowledge, academic performance, and motivation levels. The students who received SERT training attended a 2-hour training session. At the beginning of the session, students received instruction about the process of self-explanation and the comprehension strategies with examples of each strategy in Table 4.4.

Then, the students watched a video of another student self-explaining a text about forest fires. The instructor stopped at four predetermined points in the video and asked all of the students to write down the strategies the student in the video had been using to self-explain the text. After all of the students had done so, the instructor led a discussion concerning which strategies were used.

After the video was completed, the students were given two texts to self-explain in groups of two. Thus, in pairs, the students took turns self-explaining each paragraph of the text. After one student had self-explained each sentence of an entire paragraph, the second student summarized that paragraph. The second student then self-explained the following paragraph, and so on.

The main question in this study was whether the SERT training would affect the students' exam performance. The students in both groups took three exams over the duration of their biology course. Performance on the exams for students who did receive SERT training was compared to those who did not. Notably, the results showed that when students had more knowledge about science before the course began, the SERT training was *not* beneficial (for their exam performance in that course). Their performance on the exams varied between 74% and 82% regardless of whether they had received SERT training. Thus, high-knowledge students benefited less from SERT in this course because their prior knowledge was activated automatically, and they did not need to explain the material in order to understand it.

By contrast, the results for the low-knowledge students are shown in Figure 4.4. These results show that the low-knowledge students in the biology course benefited throughout the duration of the course from the brief 2-hour SERT training. As can be seen in Figure 4.4, low-knowledge students who received the SERT training showed better performance on all three exams.

It is important to note that although the benefits of SERT remained significant on the last exam, they were less pronounced. And so, incorporating these strategies into the classroom on a regular basis across multiple study episodes, rather than just at the start of the term, should help to sustain their benefits. Nonetheless, this study demonstrates that a 2-hour session in SERT training with a topic unrelated to their course helped low-knowledge students learn how to self-explain content in their course, which led to better performance on their course exams.

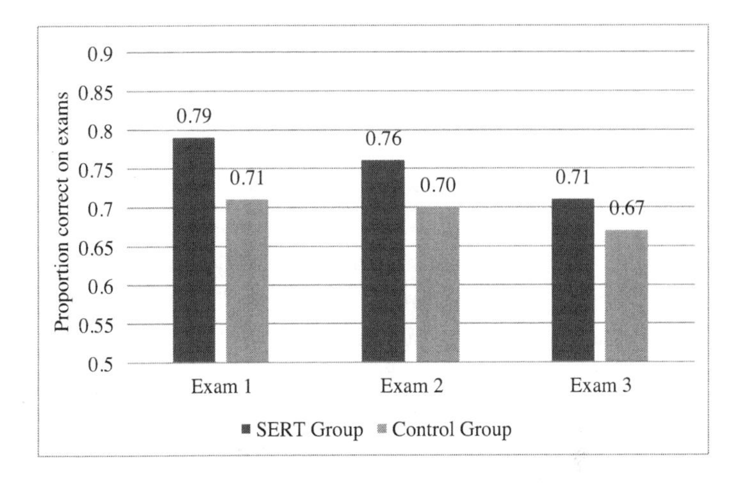

Figure 4.4 The results from McNamara[23] show that low-knowledge students who received SERT training performed significantly better than low-knowledge students who did not receive SERT training on all three exams, and performed as well as the high-knowledge students. (*The results are reported in terms of the proportion correct on the course exams*)

These studies show that self-explanation training effectively improves comprehension and course performance for university students with low prior knowledge. But what about younger students? Indeed, there are several studies that have demonstrated the benefits of providing self-explanation training to adolescent students (12 years of age and above). In one such study conducted by Tenaha O'Reilly, Rachel Best, and Danielle McNamara,[24] students from an inner-city high school received strategy training in their biology courses. There were three types of training. Students who received *SERT* training received the same training as described earlier that was provided for university students in another study by McNamara[23]. Students who received *preview* training were taught to preview subsections of a text (e.g., title, introduction, italicized words, conclusions), and strategies for taking notes while reading using questions such as What I know, What I need to know, and What I found out (i.e., similar to K-W-L: Know, Want to know, Learned). Previewing involves activating prior knowledge before reading the text. As in the SERT group, an experimenter demonstrated the strategies to the students, and then the students practiced using the techniques on a chapter from their textbook. Students who received *no training* (i.e., the control group) simply wrote down the strategies that they used while reading text, but they did not discuss the strategies.

To assess the effects of the training on students' ability to understand challenging text, students read a science text and then answered comprehension questions both immediately after training and again one week later. For the immediate test, they read a text about viruses and answered questions immediately after the training was completed (immediate test). Then, one week after the training was completed, they read a text about earthquakes and answered questions (delayed test).

On the immediate test, scores on the comprehension questions for the three types of training did not differ. However, on the delayed test, there was a benefit for having received SERT training. The students who had received SERT training answered 43% of the comprehension questions correctly, whereas the students in the Preview and Control conditions only answered 36% correctly.

Did the effects of SERT differ for students with less knowledge about science compared to those with more knowledge? The students were also given an assessment of prior knowledge about general science (e.g., biology, earth science, physics). Based on this test, the effects of the training were examined separately for low- and high-knowledge students on the delayed

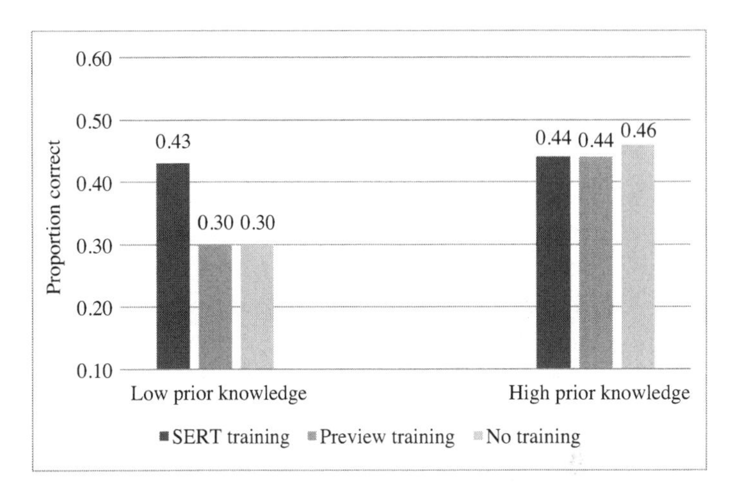

Figure 4.5 The results from O'Reilly, Best, and McNamara[24] show that low-knowledge students who were provided with SERT training performed better on the comprehension test 1-week after training compared to those in the preview and no training groups, but there was no effect of training for the high-knowledge students. (*The results are proportion of questions answered correctly out of 16. There were 8 multiple-choice questions and 8 open-ended questions*)

test. As can be seen in Figure 4.5, there were no effects of the training for the high-knowledge students. They had equivalent scores regardless of training. However, there was a substantial benefit for the low-knowledge students who had received SERT compared to students who had received preview training or no training. Previewing is not particularly effective for low-knowledge students because simply thinking about what you know is not effective if you cannot understand the material and you know very little about the content. By contrast, SERT provides students with strategies that they can use to comprehend challenging text, essentially overcoming knowledge gaps.

GRAPHIC ORGANIZERS

A third way to help students understand challenging text is to have them organize the ideas in the text in ways that scaffold the underlying meaning of the content. The order of the presentation of concepts in a text often does not align directly to the intended meaning. For example, a narrative might start at the end of the story, and then present events that led to the end. Indeed, many narratives go back and forth in time. Expository texts also require students to make connections between ideas in non-linear ways (e.g., temporal relations, hierarchical relations, compare/contrast). For some readers, tracking the structure of a text and generating alternative structures while reading is a challenging task. One way to help readers schematically organize text in a meaningful way is through the use of graphic organizers (i.e., visual displays that show relationships between facts, concepts, or other ideas).

There are several advantages of graphic organizers. One is the ability to represent relatively complex non-linear relations among concepts in the text. Also, representing the text contents graphically or visually helps readers reorganize concepts in more meaningful ways. Graphic organizers also externalize the ideas in the text and require the reader to generate information and connect the new information to prior knowledge.

Completing a Graphic Organizer Is Beneficial for Learning!

An effective graphic organizer can be used to organize important ideas and show how those ideas are related. There are three main ways that verbal information can be organized in a graphic organizer: sequence, hierarchy, and matrix (see Table 4.5).

A sequence uses arrows to show steps, events, stages, or phases in a temporally ordered process (see Figure 4.6), such as steps in the transformation of a caterpillar into a butterfly.

Table 4.5 Main types of graphic organizers

Type of graphic organizer	*Sequence*	*Hierarchy*	*Matrix*
Type of relations displayed	Temporal	Hierarchical	Relational
Definition of types of relations displayed	Chronological ordering of steps, events, stages, or phases	Structural relations (i.e., superordinate and subordinate) between concepts	Comparisons between facts/ concepts

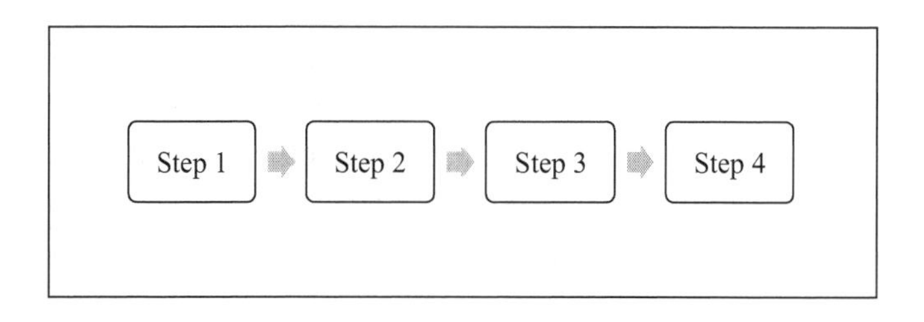

Figure 4.6 Sequence

A hierarchy uses branches to display concepts on the basis of super- and sub-ordinate conceptual levels (see Figure 4.7).

A matrix (see Figure 4.8) is a two-dimensional table that is organized vertically by topic (e.g., artery or vein) and horizontally by category (e.g., thickness, elasticity, and function).

A study by Hector Ponce and Richard Mayer[25] illustrates the benefits of generating verbal information for a computer-based *matrix* organizer. In their study, the students read a *compare and contrast* text passage presented on a computer, which summarized the differences between eastern-style and western-style steamboats. Students were randomly assigned

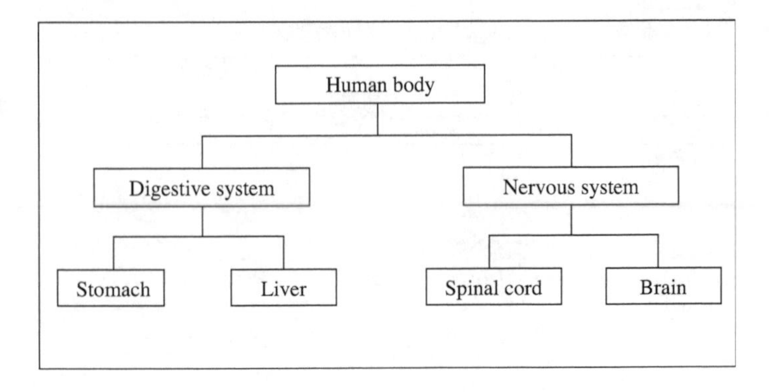

Figure 4.7 Hierarchy

	Arteries	**Veins**
Comparative Thickness	Thicker	Thinner
Comparative Elasticity	More elastic	Less elastic
Function	Carry blood away from heart	Carry blood to heart

Figure 4.8 Matrix

to one of three groups. Students in the *read-only* group read the text twice. Students in the *notepad* group took notes using an online notepad. The note-taking tool was displayed next to the text passage and enabled students to type notes. Students in the *matrix* group took notes using an online matrix, which is designed to help students compare and contrast ideas. The matrix was displayed next to the text passage, and enabled students to type notes. Students in the notepad and matrix groups were not able to copy-and-paste information from the text passage into their notes. After all students finished reading the passage, they each wrote a summary of the passage followed by a sentence completion test (e.g., 'The eastern steamboats used ________ engines'; the missing word that students needed to write to complete the sentence was 'low-pressure.'). The summary task measured students' ability to build connections between ideas, and the sentence completion task measured students' memory for the text passage.

If generating verbal information is more beneficial for learning, then the notepad and matrix groups should outperform the read-only group. Further, if the organization of the note-taking tool is important, then the matrix group should outperform the notepad group because the matrix should help students more easily compare and contrast the two types of steamships that were described in the text passage.

There were two main findings. First, the matrix and notepad groups outperformed the read-only group on both the sentence completion and summary tasks (see Figure 4.9). Second, the matrix group outperformed the notepad group on the summary task, but not on the sentence-completion task (although the matrix group had higher scores numerically, the difference was not statistically significant on the sentence-completion task). Thus, these results showed that generating verbal information promoted memory for information, and that the organization of the note-taking tool further promoted learning of compare/contrast relations. This latter finding highlights the notion that the organization of a graphic organizer helps students learn relations between important ideas, and in particular that a matrix helps students learn compare/contrast relations. Specifically, a matrix note-taking tool can aid students in selecting and processing relevant information. Further, the organization of a matrix allows students to readily make comparisons between concepts. So, having related ideas side-by-side allows students to focus on concepts and hold them in working memory, allowing them to

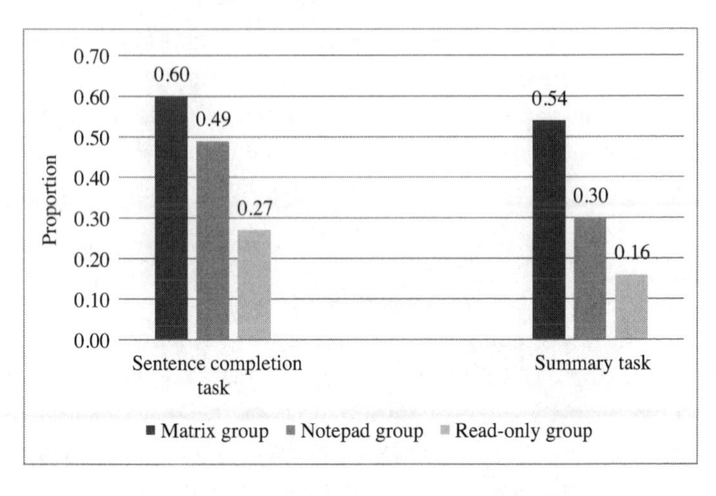

Figure 4.9 The results from Ponce and Mayer[25] show that generating verbal information promotes memory for information (see sentence completion task data), and that the organization of a note-taking tool further promotes learning of compare/contrast relations (see summary task data). For the summary task, students could compare the two steamboats along nine dimensions (e.g., engine type). To receive one point, students had to make a complete comparison (e.g., "the engines were low-pressure in eastern boats and high-pressure in western boats"). (*The results for the sentence completion task are presented in terms of the proportion of words recalled out of 13, and for the summary task, it is the proportion out of 9 points*)

build connections between ideas, as well as connections in long-term memory.

Completing a sequence organizer has similar benefits to completing a matrix organizer. However, a *sequence* organizer allows students to identify temporal connections between ideas. A study by Matt McCrudden, Montana McCormick, and Erin McTigue[26] shows the benefit of generating verbal information for a paper-based sequence organizer. University students read a text passage that described the human heart's anatomy and the order in which blood flows through the circulatory system. Their task was to identify key anatomical features of the heart from the text and to write them on their respective organizers that reflected the order of blood flow. There were three different kinds of organizers and students were randomly assigned to one of three groups.

Students in the *list* group used the text to complete a numbered list of definitions of the circulatory system's components (see Figure 4.10). Their task was to write the term next to its definition.

Students in the *sequence* group completed a sequence organizer while they studied. The organizer consisted of empty boxes that were connected by arrows (see Figure 4.11). Their task was to select the terms from the text that coincided with the empty box and to write the term in the box.

Students in the *picture* group viewed a drawing of the human heart with numbered, blank lines for inserting the labels onto the organizer (see Figure 4.12). Their task was to select the term from the text that coincided with the line of the drawing and to write the term on the line.

After they studied their respective materials, students completed a blood flow test and an oxygenation test. For the blood flow test, students were given a word bank of terms from the reading and were asked to present the blood flow sequence in the correct order using the terms from the word bank. For the oxygenation test, students received a list of 19 locations in the circulatory system and were asked to indicate whether blood at each location was oxygenated.

The results showed that the sequence and picture groups outperformed the list group on both the blow flow test and the oxygenation test (see Figure 4.13). Generating information for the sequence or the picture helped students to understand and remember the information from the text passage better

1a. ___________________—vein in the upper right part of the heart that delivers blood from the upper body to the right atrium

1b. ___________________—vein in the lower right part of the heart that delivers blood from the lower body to the right atrium

2. ___________________—chamber in the upper right part of the heart that receives blood from the vena cava

3. ___________________—chamber in the lower right part of the heart that receives blood from the right atrium

4. ___________________—arteries that begin at the right ventricle and carry blood to both lungs

5. Lungs (right & left)___—where the blood drops off carbon dioxide and picks up fresh oxygen

6. ___________________—veins that begin at the lungs and carry blood to the left atrium

7. ___________________—chamber in the upper left part of the heart that receives blood from the pulmonary veins

8. ___________________—chamber in the lower left part of the heart that receives blood from the left atrium

9. ___________________—artery that begins at the left ventricle and delivers blood to the aortic arch and descending aorta

10a. ___________________—part of the aorta in the upper part of the heart that delivers blood to the upper body

10b. ___________________—part of the aorta in the lower part of the heart that delivers blood to the lower body

Figure 4.10 List organizer

than generating information for the list. However, the differences between the sequence and picture groups were not statistically significant.

These findings again highlight the notion that the organization of a graphic organizer helps students learn relations

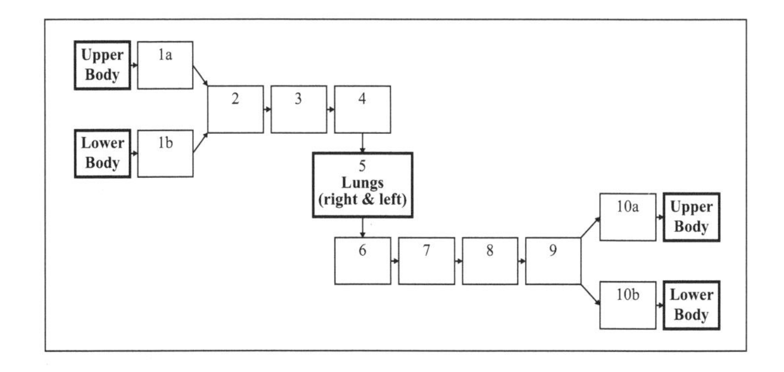

Figure 4.11 Sequence organizer

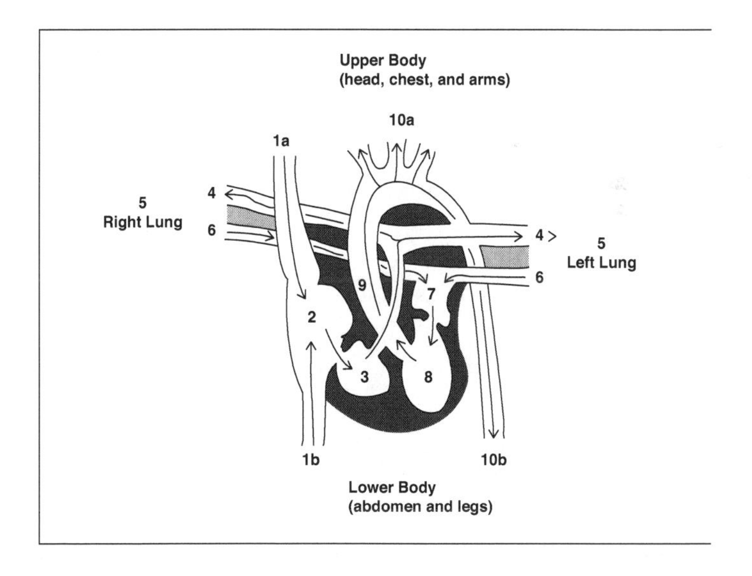

Figure 4.12 Picture organizer

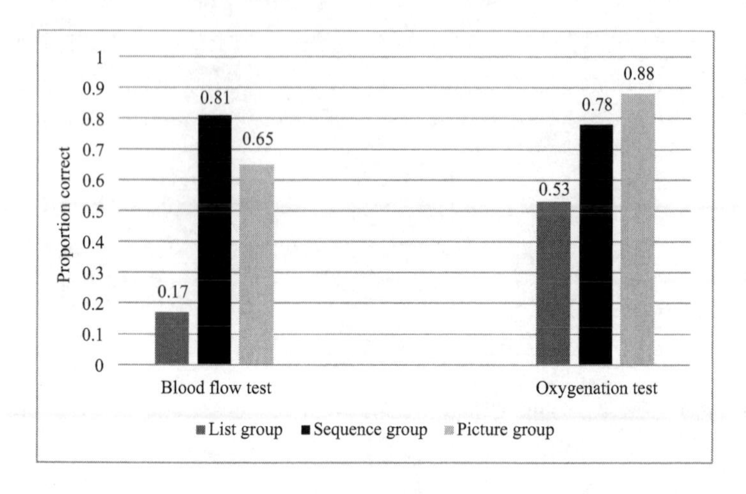

Figure 4.13 The results from McCrudden, McCormick, and McTigue[26] show that generating verbal information for a sequence or picture organizer promotes memory for temporal relations, and that the organization of an organizer further promotes learning of temporal relations. (*The results for the blood flow test are presented in terms of the proportion of correct steps in the sequence out of 15, and the results for the oxygenation test are presented in terms of the proportion of correct responses out of 19*)

between important ideas, and in particular that a sequence helps students learn temporal relations. Specifically, a sequence note-taking tool in which students generate information to be placed in the sequence organizer can help students focus their attention on relevant information. Further, the organization of a sequence allows students to readily see connections between steps in a sequence. Seeing related ideas side-by-side allows students to focus on concepts and hold them in working memory, allowing them to build connections between ideas. But, the graphic organizer was not better than providing the students with the visual display of the heart. The students' active integration of the text and the picture is a crucial component of comprehension because text/picture integration is sometimes quite challenging. Directing students' attention to the organizer or picture and having them generate the labels was likely a key ingredient to improving performance.

Improving Comprehension: Student Perspective

As a student, you may encounter challenging text often during your studies. It's crucial that you monitor your comprehension, and maintain the drive to understand text despite the obstacles you face.

Have the Drive to Comprehend the Text That You Read!

When you don't automatically understand text, it's important that you attempt to use comprehension strategies such as those we've presented here. You might remember these techniques using the mnemonic **AEO**, for *Ask*, *Explain*, *Organize*. These three techniques, combined with a mindfulness to use comprehension strategies to elaborate and make connections (or bridges) between ideas in the text, will take you far.

Asking deep meaningful questions, such as *how* and *why* questions, takes practice. Likewise, answering such questions involves persistence and resourcefulness. You might use outside sources such as your teacher, friend, or the Internet, but it is most effective if you generate an explanation yourself. Generating an explanation helps you to create a coherent understanding of the text and to understand the underlying relations between ideas in the text. But self-explanation takes practice; so you need to be mindful of explaining text whenever you encounter obstacles in your comprehension.

Also, be mindful of using the comprehension strategies presented in Table 4.4. Paraphrase the text into your own words while you are reading and make links between the ideas within the text (bridging) and to what you already know (elaboration). Importantly, self-explanation provides a vehicle for externalizing those strategies, or making them more explicit.

Finally, there are several ways to maximize the benefits of using visual and graphic organizers. First, you can link information from the text to visual displays. One way to do this is to identify visual displays from your text or other learning materials, such as your class notes, and then recreate them. Remember that it is important to actively generate connections between the text and the visual display—this does not happen automatically!

Another approach is to develop your own visual displays. To do this, it is important to align the type of organizer with the type of relations that you intend to represent. A sequence diagram helps you identify temporal relations. A hierarchy helps you see structural relations. A matrix helps you see comparisons. Not only does generating a visual organizer help you learn the information, it can serve as a study tool for later. For instance, as a form of retrieval practice, you can attempt to recall information from memory to complete an empty or partially-empty organizer.

Improving Comprehension: Teacher Perspective

Comprehension strategies are essential to learning from text. It's important to remember that students often do not understand the text that they read, and comprehension strategies can help them to construct coherent understandings. It is also important to understand that telling students to use strategies without practice or feedback is not effective. It is crucial that the students practice using the strategies.

The amount of instruction and practice that is necessary for students to learn these strategies depends on their developmental stage and their reading skill. Younger students, for example, benefit from question stems that can be used for a wide variety of subject domains, such as:

- What does the author intend by ___________?
- Why does the author say_________?
- Explain why _________?
- How is ______related to_____?
- How does ______compare/contrast with _____?
- What would happen if_______?

Question stems such as these and other types of questions are beneficial because they activate prior knowledge in long-term memory, support active processing, and foster comprehension monitoring. Question generation also induces the reader to go beyond the text. Generating questions forces the reader to think about what is already known and what needs to be learned from the text.

As a teacher, you can also attempt to use the following practices in order to maximize the benefits of explanations. Be mindful that explanations are more beneficial when they are student-generated than when they are provided to students. This can be a challenge in a classroom—when students ask questions, it's natural to answer them. But it can be more beneficial if you either have the students attempt to answer their own questions (perhaps with prompts or hints) or to have other students in the class answer and elaborate on the questions. This takes time and patience but can pay off large dividends.

Nonetheless, there may be cases when students struggle to explain how ideas are related. What can be done in these situations?

- Ask guiding questions
- Use cognitive modeling (i.e., the model verbally explains his/her thoughts while doing some task)
- Use visual displays

You can also make question asking and explanation a part of a community of practice in the classroom. This can be achieved in a classroom in numerous ways. For example, the students could be placed in pairs and asked to take turns self-explaining a portion of the textbook. The teacher can also have the students self-explain as a class—calling on students to begin or continue self-explanations and asking the students to write out self-explanations for selected sentences in text. These simple exercises may have important benefits, particularly for the struggling students.

Much like comprehension strategies, students need practice using and creating visual displays. For instance, younger students may be less familiar with how to read different kinds of visual displays. So, it is helpful to explain how to interpret a visual display and to use cognitive modeling to show students how to use or create displays. It is also important to communicate to students that different types of displays are designed to show different types of relations, such as a matrix can effectively show compare and contrast relations.

In sum, teachers need to incorporate comprehension strategies into the daily practice of the classroom. Sometimes, teachers have even stopped using text in classrooms when they observe the difficulties that students have when they read challenging text—textbooks that may be provided without consideration of students' prior knowledge. It's important to not give up. Students benefit from reading text to learn challenging concepts and it's important that students learn *how to learn* from challenging expository text. Reading and discussing text, working through challenging text, asking questions and generating explanations, are all important classroom practices that help students learn that they can tackle difficult content and challenging texts.

IMPROVING COMPREHENSION: SUMMARY OF KEY IDEAS

1. Text is often challenging and students often lack sufficient prior knowledge to comprehend challenging text.
2. Generating questions, elaborating or explaining text, and completing graphic organizers are effective in improving students' understanding of challenging text across multiple age levels and multiple types of texts.
3. Students can generate questions before, during, and after reading a text.
4. Generating high-quality questions benefits comprehension.
   a. Students may need practice and **scaffolding** to learn how to generate high-quality questions.
   b. It is also important that students learn to formulate responses to their questions.
5. Generating elaborations and explanations is beneficial to comprehending and learning from text.
   a. When the text is very challenging, students need scaffolding (i.e., assistance that helps learners do a task that they would not likely be able to do independently) and practice to generate high-quality self-explanations.
   b. Self-explanation reading training (SERT) improves explanation quality, text comprehension, and course performance.
6. Graphic organizers and visual displays can represent relatively complex non-linear relations among concepts in the text.
7. Completing a graphic organizer is beneficial for learning from text.
   a. There are three main ways that verbal information can be organized in a visual display: sequence, hierarchy, and matrix.

b. Having related ideas side-by-side allows students to focus on concepts and build connections between ideas and to long-term memory.
c. It is important to align the type of display with the type of relations that align with the text as well as the comprehension or learning objectives.

CONCLUSIONS

Our goal in writing this book was to provide a brief, digestible overview of cognition, with a specific focus on the three aspects of cognition (attention, memory, and comprehension) that we view as fundamental to learning. We focused on providing students and teachers with evidence-based strategies and techniques that are beneficial for learning. We did not discuss all of the strategies and techniques in the literature that can improve memory—we only focused on a few that have strong empirical support, are relatively easy to implement in the classroom, and require little or no financial cost. As such, they can be used by most students and teachers.

To improve attention, we focused on making information salient to students. They are more likely to attend to information that is novel, emotion-eliciting, physically distinct, or relevant. Task-orienting instructions can be used to make information relevant, such as answering prequestions before reading or instruction, which prompt students to retrieve what they already know about the topic.

To improve memory, we focused on distributing study across multiple study episodes, and on retrieving (or testing) information from memory multiple times. Both of these rely on generating to-be-learned information when it is not available in working memory—retrieving it from memory.

To improve comprehension, we focused on three strategies: asking questions, elaborating and explaining, and using graphic organizers. Across all three strategies, the focus is on improving comprehension when the material is particularly challenging (when you know little about the topic) and on generating links between ideas within the text and to prior knowledge about the domain, and also to general, world knowledge.

We included topics that we believe show the most effective, interesting, and sometimes un-intuitive strategies and techniques that support human learning across ages, settings, and content. For instance, before reading this book, were you aware that retrieval practice not only helps you assess what you have learned, but that the act of retrieval itself is a powerful tool that strengthens memory?

Some of these ideas will be well-received, other less well-received, and still others will be resisted. For example, if you (or your students) have been using rote rehearsal regularly, using distributed practice or retrieval practice involves a change from the known. And, when students are preparing for graded tests or other assignments, they like to keep doing what they've already been doing. This is why it is so important to practice these strategies and techniques on a regular basis.

As with all skills, learning to use a strategy takes practice. Think back to when you were learning swim. Your parents didn't begin by throwing you into the deep end of the pool (hopefully). You started in the shallow end, learned how to put your head under water, how to float, and move your arms and legs, and eventually these skills were brought together to swim a few strokes, then later to swim longer distances. Learning to swim, which involves procedural knowledge, takes time and practice, in much the same way that learning how to use learning strategies and techniques takes time and practice.

Teaching students to use strategies involves (1) introducing, modeling, and describing the strategy, (2) explaining why the strategy is effective, (3) discussing when to use the strategy, and (4) providing practice in using the strategy. Devoting class time to teaching students how to learn shows students that you place value on these powerful strategies. Keep in mind the following proverb: '*Give* a man a fish and you feed him for a day. *Teach* a man to fish and you feed him for a lifetime.'

Of course, teaching involves more than just a focus on learning strategies. It is a complex process that occurs in a dynamic environment. It is a social process. It involves collaboration between the instructor and students, and between the students themselves. There are techniques to improve those social interactions and methods to enhance learning by capitalizing on those social interactions, but we did not discuss those here because our focus is on individual cognition—what the student can do individually. And, as you have seen, the individual student can be a powerful force in improving memory and comprehension!

We are indebted to the many researchers and educators across the past century who have dedicated their efforts toward developing and testing methods to improve learning and comprehension. We are indebted to the teachers and students who have participated in those studies. Based on those studies, we are confident that memory and learning can be improved, for all students. Our most sincere hope is that you find the information and recommendations that we have provided useful, effective, and empowering.

ADDITIONAL READINGS

Dunlosky, J., Rawson, K. A., Marsh, E. J., Nathan, M. J., & Willingham, D. T. (2013). Improving students' learning with effective learning techniques: Promising directions from cognitive and educational psychology. *Psychological Science in the Public Interest*, 14, 4–58.

Kiewra, K. A. (2005). *Learn how to study and SOAR to success*. Upper Saddle Creek, NJ: Pearson Prentice Hall.

McCrudden, M. T., Magliano, J., & Schraw, G. (Eds.). (2011). *Text relevance and learning from text*. Charlotte, NC: Information Age Publishing.

McCrudden, M. T., & Rapp, D. N. (in press). How visual displays affect cognitive processing. *Educational Psychology Review*.

McNamara, D. S. (Ed.). (2007). *Reading comprehension strategies: Theory, interventions, and technologies*. Mahwah, NJ: Erlbaum.

Oakhill, J., Cain, K., & Elbro, C. (2014). *Understanding and teaching reading comprehension: A handbook*. London: Routledge.

Putnam, A. L., Sungkhasettee, V. W., & Roediger, H. L. (2016). Optimizing learning in college: Tips from cognitive psychology. *Perspectives on Psychological Science*, *11*, 652–660.

ACKNOWLEDGMENTS

We are grateful to our students, research assistants, and family who support us in our research and lives. We particularly thank Lauren Van Noorden and two reviewers for their feedback on earlier drafts. The writing of this book was supported in part by the Institute of Education Sciences (R305A130124 and R305A120707) and the Office of Naval Research (N00014140343). Any opinions or conclusions expressed are those of the authors and do not represent views of the IES or ONR.

Glossary

Accessibility—the extent to which information is retrievable from long-term memory.

AEO—mnemonic for *Ask*, *Explain*, *Organize*, which refers to three general comprehension strategies (ask/generate questions, explain ideas, organize information to show relationships).

Attention—our ability to focus on specific stimuli, ideas, or events for further processing in working memory.

Autobiographical memory—memory that originates from the joint contribution of semantic and episodic memory.

Availability—whether information is present in memory.

Cohesion—the extent to which a text includes overlapping words and concepts between sentences and paragraphs (cohesion affects our ability to understand text and is particularly important to content that is unfamiliar).

Cognition—cognitive processes or mental actions that affect how our minds function.

Declarative memory—memory for stating and using facts and concepts (a type of long-term memory).

Desirable difficulty—a difficulty is considered to be desirable when the challenge associated with doing a task supports learning. For example, a free recall for retrieval practice is more difficult than cued recall or recognition, but free recall as a form of retrieval practice supports long-term learning better.

Distributed practice—using a study schedule in which you spread out study episodes over time.

Distributed practice effect—people learn better when they spread their study across multiple periods of time (also known as the spacing effect).

Elaborative rehearsal—thinking about the meaning of information as opposed to rote rehearsal which involves verbatim repetition.

Emotional content—information or experiences that elicit strong feelings.

Encoding—the processes we use to transform information into a memory representation, which can then be retained in long-term memory; encoding involves the use of our current experiences to create new memories.

Episodic memory—memory for personal experiences or events (a type of declarative long-term memory).

Explanation—clarifying the significance or meaning of the facts in relation to each other (explaining how ideas are related).

Explicit procedural memory—a type of procedural memory that consists of actions you can describe, such as solving a math problem or writing the letter "A" (see also declarative memory).

Free recall—recall for ideas wherein the ideas can be recalled in any order and there are no cues provided (i.e., contrasted with cued-recall in which cues are provided).

Graphic organizers—visual displays (e.g., sequence, hierarchy, and matrix) that show relationships between facts, concepts, or other ideas.

Implicit procedural memory—a type of procedural memory that consists of actions you can perform but are difficult to verbally explain, such as balancing on a bike or floating while swimming.

Learning—a change in knowledge that occurs after we encounter new information or have a new experience.

Limited capacity assumption—the assumption that only a limited amount of information can be in our focus of attention at any given time.

Limited duration assumption—the assumption that there is a time limit for how long we can maintain and process information in conscious awareness without continually rehearsing the information.

Long-term memory—the memory system that we use to retain information, including declarative and procedural memory, for long periods of time, such as days, weeks, and even years.

Metacognition—knowledge of cognition (what individuals know about cognition) and regulation of cognition (actions we do to guide thinking and learning).

Novelty—the extent to which some stimuli are more distinct than others.

Physical properties—features of stimuli that are used to describe their appearance, such as contrast, color, and movement.

Prior knowledge—knowledge or ideas already known before we encounter new information.

Procedural memory—memory for performing actions or skills (a type of long-term memory).

Readability—how easily a reader can understand a text. Readability is generally based on formulas that combine measures to estimate the difficulty of the words and sentences.

Relevance—the extent to which information is useful to a person's goals.

Retrieval—the activation of information that is already retained in long-term memory.

Retrieval practice—attempting to retrieve information from memory.

Retrieval practice effect—people learn better when they use their study time attempting to retrieve information from memory rather than re-reading information.

Rote rehearsal—verbatim repetition of information.

Scaffolding—assistance that helps learners do a task that they would *not* likely be able to do independently.

Self-explanation—an explanation that is directed toward oneself, with the express purpose of constructing the meaning of the text.

Self-explanation reading training (SERT)—training to explain the meaning of information to oneself while reading while using comprehension strategies, including comprehension monitoring, paraphrasing, elaborating, and making bridging inferences.

Semantic memory—memory for general knowledge of the world (a type of declarative long-term memory).

Sensory memory—the memory system that passively detects environmental stimuli that impact our senses for a brief amount of time (i.e., two seconds or less) and allows us to transform our sensory experiences into meaningful forms.

Task-orienting instructions—instructions that are provided to students when they are asked to do assigned tasks; they are meant to communicate the requirements or expectations of the assigned task.

Working memory—the memory system that we use to consciously hold and process information for short periods of time (i.e., about 20 seconds).

References

1. McNamara, D. S. (Ed.). (2007). *Reading comprehension strategies: Theory, interventions, and technologies*. Mahwah, NJ: Erlbaum.
2. Crossley, S. A., & McNamara, D. S. (Eds.). (2016). *Adaptive educational technologies for literacy instruction*. New York: Taylor & Francis, Routledge.
3. Cherry, E. C. (1953). Some experiments on the recognition of speech, with one and with two ears. *The Journal of the Acoustical Society of America*, 25(5), 975–979.
4. Strayer, D. L., Drews, F. A., & Johnston, W. A. (2003). Cell phone induced failures of visual attention during simulated driving. *Journal of Experimental Psychology: Applied*, 9, 23–52.
5. Bosker, H. R., Tjiong, V., Quené, H., Sanders, T., & De Jong, N. H. (2015). Both native and non-native disfluencies trigger listeners' attention. In Disfluency in Spontaneous Speech: DISS 2015: An ICPhS Satellite Meeting. Edinburgh: DISS2015.
6. McCrudden, M. T., Magliano, J. P., & Schraw, G. (2010). Exploring how relevance instructions affect personal reading intentions, reading goals, and text processing: A mixed methods study. *Contemporary Educational Psychology*, 35, 229–241.
7. Pressley, M., Tanenbaum, R., McDaniel, M. A., & Wood, E. (1990). What happens when university students try to answer prequestions that accompany textbook material? *Contemporary Educational Psychology*, 15, 27–35.
8. Carpenter, S. K., & Toftness, A. R. (2016). The effect of prequestions on learning from video presentations. *Journal of Applied Research in Memory and Cognition*, 6, 104–109.
9. Bloom, K. C., & Shuell, T. J. (1981). Effects of massed and distributed practice on the learning and retention of second-language vocabulary. *Journal of Educational Research*, 74, 245–248.

10. Dempster, F. N. (1987). Effects of variable encoding and spaced presentations on vocabulary learning. *Journal of Educational Psychology, 79,* 162–170.
11. Rohrer, D., & Taylor, K. (2006). The effects of overlearning and distributed practice on the retention of mathematics knowledge. *Applied Cognitive Psychology, 20,* 1209–1224.
12. Kornell, N., & Bjork, R. A. (2008). Learning, concepts, and categories: Is spacing the "enemy of induction?" *Psychological Science, 19,* 585–592.
13. Roediger, H. L., III, & Karpicke, J. D. (2006). Test-enhanced learning: Taking memory tests improves long-term retention. *Psychological Science, 17,* 249–255.
14. Glover, J. A. (1989). The "testing" phenomenon: Not gone but nearly forgotten. *Journal of Educational Psychology, 81,* 392–399.
15. Butler, A. C., & Roediger, H. L., III. (2007). Testing improves long-term retention in a simulated classroom setting. *European Journal of Cognitive Psychology, 19,* 514–527.
16. Pyc, M. A., & Rawson, K. A. (2009). Testing the retrieval effort hypothesis: Does greater difficulty correctly recalling information lead to higher levels of memory? *Journal of Memory and Language, 60,* 437–447.
17. Rosenshine, B., Meister, C., & Chapman, S. (1996). Teaching students to generate questions: A review of the intervention studies. *Review of Educational Research, 66,* 181–221.
18. Cohen, R. (1983). Students generate questions as an aid to reading comprehension. *Reading Teacher, 36,* 770–777.
19. Davey, B., & McBride, S. (1986). Effects of question-generation on reading comprehension. *Journal of Educational Psychology, 78,* 256–262.
20. Pressley, M., McDaniel, M. A., Turnure, J. E., Wood, E., & Ahmad, M. (1987). Generation and precision of elaboration: Effects on intentional and incidental learning. *Journal of Experimental Psychology: Learning, Memory, and Cognition, 13,* 291–300.
21. McNamara, D. S. (2004). SERT: Self-explanation reading training. *Discourse Processes, 38*(1), 1–30.
22. Palincsar, A. S., & Brown, A. L. (1984). Reciprocal teaching of comprehension-fostering and comprehension-monitoring activities. *Cognition and Instruction, 2,* 117–175.
23. McNamara, D. S. (in press). Self-explanation and reading strategy training (SERT) improves low-knowledge students' science course performance. *Discourse Processes.*

24. O'Reilly, T., Best, R., & McNamara, D. S. (2004). Self-explanation reading training: Effects for low-knowledge readers. In K. Forbus, D. Gentner, & T. Regier (Eds.), *Proceedings of the 26th Annual Cognitive Science Society* (pp. 1053–1058). Mahwah, NJ: Erlbaum.
25. Ponce, H. R., & Mayer, R. E. (2014). Qualitatively different cognitive processing during online reading primed by different study activities. *Computers in Human Behavior*, 30, 121–130.
26. McCrudden, M. T., McCormick, M., & McTigue, E. (2011). Do the spatial features of an adjunct display that readers complete while reading affect their understanding of a complex system? *International Journal of Science and Mathematics Education*, 9(1), 163–185.

Index

Page numbers in italics indicate figures and tables.

Printed and bound by PG in the USA